The LIGHT Always SHINES in the Dark

Bart V. Mercurio

ISBN 979-8-89130-291-4 (paperback)
ISBN 979-8-89130-292-1 (digital)

Copyright © 2024 by Bart V. Mercurio

All rights reserved. No part of this publication may be reproduced, distributed, or transmitted in any form or by any means, including photocopying, recording, or other electronic or mechanical methods without the prior written permission of the publisher. For permission requests, solicit the publisher via the address below.

Christian Faith Publishing
832 Park Avenue
Meadville, PA 16335
www.christianfaithpublishing.com

Printed in the United States of America

For my son, Bart. He proves that regardless of the difficult trials that each of us must face during our lives, we must remain strong. We must be willing to endure. We must embrace faith and hope, and we must never stop believing that the light always shines in the dark.

Contents

Preface

The Light Always Shines in the Dark was written during a time of desolation deeply driven by a deadly virus that spread its dreadful wave of despair across America. During the unforeseen COVID-19 pandemic, lives of millions of men and women were affected in many ways. One of the most devastating effects was triggered by the scourge of pornography, a multibillion-dollar industry that corrupts souls, destroys relationships, and ruthlessly exploits the horrible crime of human trafficking.

The Light Always Shines in the Dark, a thought-provoking and inspirational follow-up to *At Last I Open My Heart,* examines a wide range of social issues. Though the topics are presented from a worldview based on a biblical perspective, the thoughts, feelings, and ideas expressed should broadly appeal to the interest of Christian and secular audiences alike.

Each day that we celebrate on this earth is yet another reminder of the extraordinary miracle of life that we have been granted. We must cherish the priceless virtues of faith and love, and despite the ominous shadow of darkness that continues to engulf our lives, we must hope and pray for a brighter future and take comfort in genuinely believing that the light will always shine in the dark.

1

Faith Over Fear

> Through him all things were made; without him
> nothing was made that has been made.
> In him was life, and that life was the light of all mankind.
> The light shines in the darkness, and the
> darkness has not overcome the light.

> —John 1:3–5

Towering high above the huge crowd, the giant, glowing ball methodically started its annual descent in New York City's Times Square. Deafening cheers reverberated through the cold, evening air as the final ten seconds ticked away during the traditional countdown that would soon welcome America into the 2020 new year. As the brightly lit ball dropped snugly into its designated spot, no one among the thousands of spectators reveling that evening might have possibly guessed that in just a few short weeks, a deadly virus would come sweeping into their nation like the fury of a category four hurricane, a pandemic of such severity that had not been witnessed in more than one hundred years, not since the Spanish flu had infected more than one third of the earth's population and tragically ended the lives of nearly fifty million people worldwide.

On a calm, humid, Sunday evening, nine months after the unexpected arrival of the deadly coronavirus, I silently observed my seventy-seventh birthday. Struck by the thought that I had already journeyed more than halfway into the eighth decade of my life, I wondered in disbelief how all of those years had passed me by so quickly. On a much more disturbing note, I became deeply concerned about a recent, public announcement reporting that eight out of ten deaths resulting from the nationwide pandemic had occurred in adults sixty-five years or older—a grim, eye-opening statistic that placed me squarely among the vulnerable group of seniors who shared an increased risk of perishing from the deadly COVID-19 virus.

In just a few months time, the unwelcome pandemic had severely fractured the entire economy. Unemployment skyrocketed. Mandatory lockdowns forced businesses, schools, and churches to abruptly close doors. While the menacing virus accelerated, spawning widespread despair and hopelessness among millions of Americans, social distancing and face masks emerged as the new norm throughout the country.

As the horrifying virus continued its terrible surge at an astronomical rate, I frequently found myself struggling with newfound fears. Not only was I at great risk of contracting the novel virus because of my advanced age but also quite vulnerable because of my personal history, which dated back to a summer morning in 1992 when I underwent triple bypass surgery because of a life-threatening diagnosis of coronary artery disease. Naturally, quite concerned about my medical history, I often found myself brooding over the likelihood of succumbing to the terrible virus.

Not until after a long bout with an untimely skin infection did I gather sufficient courage to let go of my nagging fear of COVID-19. During several, worrisome months, I was prescribed antibiotics to prevent bacterial infection from forging its way through my bloodstream. During that troublesome period, friends and relatives prayed earnestly for my recovery from the potentially fatal skin infection. After finally recuperating, I staunchly decided to no longer fear the menacing threat imposed by the frightful virus. I instead adopted a positive attitude by embracing faith over fear. For encouragement, I reminded myself of an Old Testament biblical verse that I had memorized several years earlier: "Be strong and courageous. Do not be afraid; do not be discouraged, for the lord your God will be with you wherever you go" (Joshua 1:9). I discovered additional comfort after reading a timely article entitled "Peace in a Restless Time," which presented a very promising and insightful perspective regarding the escalating, worldwide fear propagated by the frightening COVID-19 pandemic:

> We're living in a challenging, frightening, oppressive, and even depressing time. How long will this coronavirus epidemic and all of its consequences continue? Today our world seems to be like a rough sea. The weather has completely changed within a very short time. This virus has spread rapidly across the world. Fear is captivating us. Fear is visible in people's eyes. Let's not deceive ourselves: as Christians, we too are also adrift on this troubled sea. We are also afraid.
>
> Now that public life has mostly come to a standstill—schools, movie theaters, and many shops have been closed; events have been prohibited; and people who are sick and elderly remain at home—now we should have the time that God has given us to reflect, to calm down and to search through our Bibles for the consolation, confidence, encouragement, hope, strengthening, and yes, peace and joy that we all need.[1]

After reading "Peace in a Restless Time," I was thoroughly convinced not to waver from my positive attitude of faith over fear. Soon afterward, I tossed around the idea of writing a sequel to *At Last I Open My Heart*,[2] an autobiographical account of my remarkable recovery from a decades-long struggle with sexual addiction. As I learned more and more about the harmful and abundant use of pornography and especially its devastating effects on millions of men and women during the COVID-19 pandemic, I unhesitatingly decided that writing a sequel to my first book would be more timely than ever.

Pornography is a thriving, global, multibillion-dollar industry that evolves into something more violent and degrading each day. It crushes innocent souls and destroys marriages, families, and relationships. It sadly and tragically feeds human sex trafficking across the globe. Never should its use be casually underestimated or dismissed as a form of harmless behavior. It can easily seduce any man or woman in the blink of an eye.

In "How Big Porn is Making the Coronavirus Crisis Even Worse,"[3] which appeared in The Federalist, a web magazine that focuses on culture, politics, and religion, several startling observations are offered in connection with the harmful link between pornography and the COVID-19 pandemic:

> The Wuhan coronavirus epidemic has turned the lives of most Americans completely upside down. As social distancing practices have been adopted nationwide, many have found themselves isolated from everyday human interaction, suddenly cut off from extended family and friends, and—if they're lucky enough to still be employed—forced to work from home. In addition to creating a public health crisis, the virus has exacerbated a preexisting problem of loneliness and anxiety that has been plaguing many Americans, especially young men, for years…One industry in particular is taking full advantage of this crisis. The virus has provided an unprecedented opportunity for Big Porn to capitalize on our social isolation.[4]
>
> During a worldwide pandemic that has already taken thousands of lives, concerns about the rise in pornography usage may seem trivial. However, to brush these concerns aside would be

a huge mistake. Like the coronavirus, pornography use is silent yet deadly, a powerful disease that has damaging effects on our society. Although coronavirus may attract more headlines today, pornography will be with us for the longer haul. It cannot be vaccinated against and few are brave enough to stand up against it.[5]

Research has increasingly exposed the terrible consequences of widespread pornography use. To name a few: addiction to greater amounts and more depraved forms; desensitization to sexual abuse and violence; and a higher likelihood of dysfunctional relationships. Most alarming is the impact pornographic material has on children, who by some reports may encounter it for the first time as young as age eleven…The growth of the pornography industry has also led directly to the exploitation of women and children through sex trafficking. Now, more than ever, we must join together to take on the pornography industry and defeat this terrible epidemic.[6]

The production and distribution of pornography inevitably lead to disastrous consequences. In a pandemic with a magnitude of such a large scale as COVID-19, any man or woman can easily be lured into pornography's viselike grip. Scripture itself openly warns us that we can instantly be tempted when drawn or enticed by our own lust (James 1:14).

My first book, *At Last I Open My Heart*, did not soft-pedal the secret lifestyle that I once lived nor did it dismiss the deeply immoral behavior that was evidenced by a reckless life that was once replete with an ongoing streak of uncontrollable lust. My story straightforwardly tells the truth about my enslavement and how I subsequently suffered from its unfortunate consequences. Over several decades, my addiction weakened me financially and not only had a devastating effect that eventually led to the dissolution of two marriages but also transformed me into an empty, lonely, and troubled man, relentlessly searching for a genuine sense of love.

The Light Always Shines in the Dark deeply explores the seedy, lurid world in which I once thrived. It cautions about the danger and harm that results from the abusive or overabundant use of pornography, as well as its far-reaching impact during the COVID-19 pandemic. It also discusses other social issues as well—issues that are a matter of great concern in a world that seems to be swiftly plummeting into a more catastrophic direction with each passing day.

Having been redeemed by God's amazing grace, I successfully recovered from a long and harrowing addiction. I treasure these words: "Trust in the Lord with all your heart and lean not on your own understanding; in all your ways, acknowledge him, and he will make your paths straight" (Proverbs 3:5–6).

Throughout my life, I often failed to resist the temptation of sexual sin. Temptation must always be regarded as our deadly enemy, one that silently lurks in the darkness and never stops stalking our vulnerable souls. The darkness prevents the light from entering into our lives, that is, until the day that the light silently works its way into the darkness, then triumphantly overcomes it—just as it once did in my own life on a brisk, autumn morning in early November of 2001.

I am a blessed man. God has guided and protected me, safely sustaining me through decades of darkness that often reaped of lies and deception. After existing in a dark, sinful world of immorality for more than forty years, I at last successfully stepped into the light. We must always reflect on these promising words from John 1:4–5 of the New Testament: "In him was life, and the life was the light of all mankind. The light shines in the darkness, and the darkness has not overcome it."

I cherish each day that God gives me on this earth, and I will continue to believe that faith will always overcome fear, not only during the bleakness and despair of the COVID-19 pandemic but also well beyond it. I hold closely to my heart the following encouraging verse:

THE LIGHT ALWAYS SHINES IN THE DARK

When Jesus spoke again to the people, he said:

> I am the light of the world. Whoever follows
> me will never walk in darkness, but will have the
> light of life. (John 8:12)

We must live each day with assurance and hope of knowing that the light will always shine in the dark!

2

That Was Then, This Is Now

Therefore, if anyone is in Christ, he is a new creation: the old has gone, the new has come.

—2 Corinthians 5:17

I regretfully recall an unfortunate incident that occurred on a late October evening in 1974. Though it seems like the event happened just yesterday, nearly fifty years have elapsed since the Friday evening when I recklessly slipped through a cluster of suspended ceiling tiles in the men's locker room of a bowling establishment. I tumbled a distance of ten feet to the floor below. The impact of the fall seriously injured my left wrist after much of my weight struck the hard, tiled surface of the locker room floor. I have only myself to blame for that unforgettable accident because I should not have been hiding in the darkness above the ceiling panels in the first place.

That autumn evening, I made an unwise decision to gratify an unhealthy compulsion that was triggered by a foolish, criminal thought. Only one week earlier, my first marriage was sadly dissolved. At the time, intensely filled with self-hate, I viewed myself as a total failure. I had become little more than a lost soul who had gradually evolved into a full-fledged addict, and on that Friday evening, I drove myself to the borderline edge of criminal behavior.

Lying on the cold floor surrounded by fragments of twisted, aluminum metal grids and shredded pieces of plasterboard, I instinctively wondered whether or not anyone else had witnessed the careless mishap. Realizing that I was alone, I breathed a sigh of relief as I slowly rose from the floor, my left arm drooping along the side of my body in excruciating pain. I immediately noticed the distorted shape of my left wrist and guessed that I must have suffered a severe injury. As I exited the men's locker room, I tried to avoid suspicious behavior as I casually stepped into the main area of the crowded bowling establishment. Moments later, struggling to suppress the agonizing pain that had been steadily intensifying in my left arm, I found myself moving as quickly as possible toward the location of my parked car.

My arm and wrist throbbing with tremendous pain, I frantically drove toward a hospital that was about seven miles away. As I continued to battle the excruciating discomfort, I tightly gripped the steering wheel, driving cautiously with the sole use of my right arm. I arrived at the emergency room entrance of my destination shortly after midnight. An X-ray determined that I had severely broken my left wrist. Two hours later, my wrist and lower left arm were immobilized by a plaster cast that was to remain securely in place for the next seven weeks.

My motive that evening was unquestionably a very selfish one. I had criminally risked hoisting myself above an outlay of drop-down ceiling tiles in the men's locker room of a bowling establishment in an attempt to commit an act that would satisfy my lustful desires. My unsound decision was an equally disreputable one. Though nearly fifty years have gone by since that fateful evening, I have never spoken or admitted to anyone the shameful motive that eventually led to the unnecessary fracture of my wrist.

For far too long, I have struggled to cleanse my conscience from the deceptive cover-up of the deplorable incident. Back in 1974, I lied to family and friends, falsely consoling myself by sheltering my guilt and convincing others that I had simply been very careless by stumbling down a flight of steps in a building a few blocks away from my apartment. I never even disclosed the unsettling incident to my counselor during the numerous sessions that were conducted during the years that I was treated for recovery from my addiction.

I only now regretfully admit that I am deeply ashamed of the reprehensible behavior that I displayed on that unforgettable evening. Though I ultimately recovered from my long battle with addiction, a lingering and nagging thought periodically troubled me for many years. Did I have enough courage to morally cleanse my conscience from the unconfessed sin that so often haunted me? I realize that when the unfortunate event occurred I was in the wrong place at the wrong time and for the wrong reasons. I humbly repent of the unacceptable, immoral behavior and the evil intentions that swept through me that long ago evening.

Scripture reminds us (John 8:32) that the truth will set us free. I am confessing the truth so that this heavy burden may, at last be, lifted from my soul. The immoral and criminal act that I attempted to commit occurred nearly a half-century ago. That was then when I was a selfish, spiritually dead man, but this is now and as scripture assures us in Corinthians 5:17, if anyone is in Christ, he is a new creation; the old has gone and the new has come. It is no longer then. It is now. The old has gone, and the new has come.

* * * * *

On August 23, 2008, I observed my sixty-fifth birthday on a dreary Sunday afternoon in a quiet corner of the food court in Midway Mall in Elyria, Ohio. Four months had passed since the dissolution of my second marriage. Diana and I rarely communicated with each other during those months, and I often wondered whether or not she would ever communicate with me again. After sharing our lives together for fifteen years, I was faced with the reality that she tolerated far too much of my dishonesty and secrecy during our marriage. Sitting alone and brooding about an unforeseeable future, I missed Diana dearly.

My mind soon drifted back to a never-to-be-forgotten, November morning seven years earlier when Diana first learned about my hidden, immoral lifestyle. It was true that I had successfully recovered from a terrible addiction and had even commendably turned my life around before it was too late. It was also true that during my recovery, Diana and I remained together as husband and wife for six more years as we desperately tried to rebuild our broken marriage—an effort that sometimes seemed to be an insurmountable task.

I reminded myself that our marriage could have certainly been saved had it not been for my deeply rooted pride. Though Diana often reached out to forgive me, I stubbornly would not let go of my pride. Ironically, it was not the resurgence of an ugly Internet pornography habit that led to the dissolution of our marriage; more so, it was my dreadful, unyielding pride. Pride is biblically considered not only the root of all evil but perhaps one of the deadliest sins of all. In *At Last I Open My Heart*, I meticulously explain how selfish pride weighed heavily on the unfavorable outcome of our marriage:

> The chief purpose of my intended behavior was to use proceeds from hidden loans to satisfy an outstanding household debt. Certain that Diana would never agree to such a decision, I willfully refrained from informing her about my contentious course of action. My deceitful plan was little more than a disrespectful display of self-obsessed pride. By resurrecting my longtime, harmful practice of secrecy, I significantly risked the restoration of our marriage by disregarding common sense to honestly communicate with Diana, who had not only forgiven me for my past indignities but who had also continued to faithfully profess her love for me as well. Triggered by polluted pride as well as obsessive, controlling behavior, I sadly returned to the darkness of my own secret world.[7]

From the early 1960s through the late 1990s, I hopelessly existed in my own fantasy world, deeply driven by a streak of unrestrained lust and immoral behavior that often wreaked decadence and disgrace. As a spiritually dead man, my troubled heart was completely separated from the outside world, but that was then. That was before God mercifully intervened in my sinful life and allowed me an opportunity to seek redemption and a chance to recover from a debilitating and distressing addiction as well.

More than twenty years have passed since that Thursday morning in November 2001 when I was first exposed as an out-of-control addict who had been secretly living in his own world through decades of darkness. Many more years have also gone by since that summer afternoon in 2008 when I sat alone in the food court in Elyria, Ohio, pondering about an uncertain future. What I did not realize then was that only a few weeks later, I would be making a life-changing decision to share a riveting account of my long battle with addiction.

I decided that *At Last I Open My Heart* would be the title of my story. I wished to reveal the truth, not only about my harrowing addiction but also about my miraculous recovery. As I started writing the story, I was regularly haunted by my shameful and evil past, and I frequently found myself on the brink of quitting the project altogether. Though I struggled, I was determined to move forward, refusing to quit and trying my best to drive away the demons that relentlessly attacked me as I persisted with my writing. Thinking back, I feel certain that the power and the presence of the Holy Spirit served as a guiding and motivational force throughout the eleven years that were needed for me to retain the strength and courage to complete the true story about my forty-year battle with pornography and sexual addiction. The finished book was released to the public in June 2019 by Christian Faith Publishing. In summarizing the content, my own words graced the illustrated back cover of the book:

> *At Last I Open My Heart* is a compelling story about a self-destructive man who for more than forty years lived in a secret world filled with lies, lust, and deceit. It is a true account of a man who intensely hated himself and believed that his entire life was a failure. It is a moving testi-

mony about triumph and about the redemption of a once-lost soul miraculously recovering from decades of sexual addiction. It openly recognizes the seamy world of pornography, a multibillion-dollar scourge that destroys marriages and ravages relationships. No one is immune from pornography's steel grip. It is a dreadful, widespread epidemic that each day ensnares millions of men and women.

In his straightforward style, first-time author, Bart Mercurio, shamelessly takes us through the pages of his harrowing battle with pornography. He shares how his troubled heart was hidden away for nearly a half century, how he constantly lived in denial while vainly searching for genuine love, how his secret lifestyle came to be exposed, and finally how he was humbled and redeemed from his lifelong struggle with sexual addiction. His eye-opening, personal experience is inspirational and honest and delivers a powerful message that will speak loudly to every man and woman who read the story.

In chapter 12 of *At Last I Open My Heart*, "Once I Was Lost, Now I Am Found," I share in detail not only how addiction severely impacted my relationship with Diana but also how it negatively affected our marriage. I intently describe the internal conflict, self-hate, and feelings of hopelessness that frequently troubled me during a lengthy battle as a struggling addict:

Diana became a loser in our relationship because I never wanted her to experience the real me—the Bart that I would not even allow myself to experience. I convinced myself that I did not deserve to be loved by Diana, dismissing myself as an unsuitable, distrustful, worthless husband. I inflicted irrefutable harm to our marriage by my self-fulfilling prophecy that I was a total loser in life.[8]

I taught myself to believe that I only deserved intense hatred. My self-loathing attitude drove me into a false world, one that beckoned me to strive only for perfection, one that badgered me to beat myself up regularly. My life was unpropitiously impacted by a shallow belief of escaping from reality. I obsessively drove myself toward absolute perfectionism, refusing to accept personal mistakes of any kind.[9]

My fears, inadequacies, and failures were sad, but not as sad as the added grief triggered by my hiddenness. I rationalized my secrecy by believing that I could never openly trust anyone, especially God. Since I viewed myself as insecure and powerless much of the time, I sought a place where I could always remain free from rejection. I lived a self-centered life in my own fantasy world and was preoccupied with my own guilt, stubbornly and proudly unwilling to accept the responsibility to admit that I could ever be hurt in any way.[10]

Protecting a heart that was deceitful, I believed that the practice of honest behavior was a hopeless one. I refused to step out of denial to survey the enormous damage caused by my self-destructive behavior. Inwardly, I wished to never be trusted, to have no one ever really believe in me. I did not wish to succeed, and I exercised every effort to assure myself that I would fail. Sexually addicted for years, I subjected myself to incredible pain, yet managed to remain isolated from that same pain, forcing myself to believe that the pain itself never actually existed.[11]

In Romans 8:28, we find these empowering words: "God always works for the good of those who love him and who have been called according to his purpose." When my first book, *At Last I Open My Heart*, was published, I believe that God had a special plan and purpose for my life. He provided me with a firsthand testimony that could serve as an exceptional opportunity to encourage others that it is never too late to escape from the bondage of addiction.

I was once a spiritually dead man, but that was long ago. That was then. By God's amazing grace, I was redeemed. God has guided me—a once-spiritually dead man—from a dark period of evil and sin to a glorious path of redemption. He created the light to overcome the darkness that was then.

This is now, and my soul has been saved, and my heart has been transformed. This is now, and I know that the light will always shine in the dark. Hallelujah! This is now!

3

Evil That Was Meant for Good

You intended to harm me, but God intended
it for good to accomplish what is now
being done, the saving of many lives.

—Genesis 50:20

Were it not for the encouragement that I received from Geoff Schultz, senior pastor of Evangelical Friends Church in North Olmsted, Ohio, I may have not been motivated to seriously consider the opportunity to become a published author. These words appear in the closing pages of my first book, *At Last I Open My Heart*:

> After the congregation enthusiastically applauded my testimony, Pastor Geoff Schultz stepped up to the podium, thanked me for my presentation, then gently placed his hand on my shoulder, and shared a special heartwarming, introductory prayer with the congregation, fully welcoming me as a new member at North Olmsted Evangelical Friends Church. With my head bowed in prayer, I sensed a calming and reassurance of peace during those moments that I had never truly experienced during my life. I

silently rejoiced, resting assured that I had been warmly accepted into a new church home.[12]

From the first few moments that I stepped into the welcome center of North Olmsted Evangelical Friends Church in the late spring of 2015, I believed that I had finally discovered a new church home. I met with pastor Geoff Schultz shortly afterward and was welcomed as a new member six months later. I admired how Pastor Geoff would often take the time to warmly greet church members and guests following each Sunday morning service. I looked forward to his weekly sermons, which often conveyed powerful and encouraging messages that deeply reflected the empowerment of the Holy Spirit. I appreciated his communication skills as well as his presentation and interpretation of scripture.

I have often had an opportunity to share my thoughts and struggles with Pastor Geoff. He has always acknowledged my honesty and openness. I especially recall his enthusiastic response one late evening in May 2016 when I casually mentioned to him that for quite some time I had been writing a story about a lifelong struggle with addiction. He unhesitatingly expressed his genuine interest and assured me that he would very much appreciate the opportunity to read my manuscript after its completion. I consider his ongoing support and encouragement special blessings that contributed significantly to my decision to eventually attempt to publish my story. We exchanged a series of e-mail messages during the three-year period preceding the published release of *At Last I Open My Heart*. His deeply rooted interest, often expressed through the content of his messages, proved to be a vital and positive force during that transitional period. Our first communication was on September 1, 2016:

> Good evening, Geoff. Hope all is going well. A few months back I mentioned that I was writing an autobiographical account of my redemption from forty years of addiction. After nearly eleven years and with some prompting by the Holy Spirit, I've finally completed what I feel

is a satisfactory draft of the final manuscript. The story is entitled *At Last I Open My Heart.* It is a biblically based account and includes numerous references to Scripture. With regard to the nature of the subject matter, I feel that I have handled the material very appropriately. One of my main goals was to demonstrate God's amazing grace and His plan to offer redemption to a spiritually dead man whose heart was closed to the real world for most of his life. The story also clearly reveals the serious consequences that result from living a sinful life of immorality.

When we spoke about the project earlier, you expressed interest in reading it. At this point, I am looking primarily for general feedback. I know you're often busy, but if you are still interested and I hope you are, I would be more than happy to personally deliver a copy of the manuscript to you at a convenient time and place. Thanks very much for your support, Geoff, and I look forward to hearing from you soon.

Pastor Geoff commended me with his response:

Dear Bart, congratulations on reaching this point in penning your journey. I can only imagine the hours of prayer, reflection, and honest searching that went into the process…It would be my privilege to read through your manuscript. Please get it to me when you can and allow me sufficient time to read through it. I will be glad to give any input that I can…I praise God for what He has done in your life and am thankful He has called you to be part of our family at Friends.

I very much appreciated Pastor Geoff's willingness and constant support. We arranged a brief meeting at his church office the following week and I presented him with a copy of my completed manuscript. Two months later on the day before Thanksgiving, we met for a breakfast meeting at a local restaurant in North Olmsted, Ohio, to discuss my story in greater detail.

Having read the manuscript, Pastor Geoff opened our conversation by complimenting me for my courage and honesty in choosing to write a story about my lifelong struggle with sexual addiction. Toward the end of our conversation, he asked me whether I had seriously considered the possibility of trying to have my work published. I responded that I hadn't thought about that prospect at all. As it turned out that morning, his suggestion planted the seeds that over time convinced me to seek publication of my story. As we exchanged wishes for the upcoming Thanksgiving holiday, I thanked him for inviting me to breakfast and especially for his willingness to take time out to share his valuable input.

On May 9, 2018, nearly eighteen months after our breakfast meeting, I forwarded a message ecstatically announcing the wonderful news that my manuscript had been selected for publication:

> Hope you're doing well, Geoff. Just wanted to get you up to date on my story. A three-member review board at Christian Faith Publishing, based in Meadville, Pennsylvania, read my final manuscript and gave it a unanimous, resounding review, telling me that it is not only a well-written story and courageous and honest but also that it is inspirational and should impact many others who are struggling with sexual addiction. The publisher believes that my story is quite worthy of publishing and that it can be successfully marketed on a national level.
>
> I have revised the book in many areas since you first read it, adding much more information related to addiction recovery by utilizing

numerous references from books, magazines, and the Internet as well. Including that material was based primarily on much of the feedback that you provided during the breakfast we shared on that November morning in 2016. I want you to know, Geoff, that I came very close to giving up many times during the years that I labored through my writing. The Holy Spirit surely kept me going. I will always be grateful for your willingness to read my manuscript and I sincerely hope that somewhere down the road, perhaps my story might serve as an avenue to minister not only to those at Friends Church but to many other individuals and groups as well. I know you're busy, but if you get a moment to provide some feedback, I'd really appreciate it. I also ask that you continue to keep me in prayer as well. Thanks very much, Geoff, and I look forward to talking to you soon.

His reply, which arrived a few days later, complimented me on my achievement:

Good afternoon, Bart. Glad to hear that after so much work and effort a path appears to be coming clearer. As one who has never had to go through the process, I admire your tenacity and strength, never mind your courage too. It's amazing how you have continued to be open about your struggle and it only occurred to me in reading your e-mail how this may come as yet news to those who have also been very close to you. I pray that those conversations will yield fruit and understanding...

I appreciate the kindness that you've extended to me, and I certainly appreciate your trust in allowing me to read the manuscript. I'm glad to hear about your additions and revisions. That sounds like it will only enhance the power of your story. I would like to discuss with you also how in the near future we can share some of your story with our congregation. God bless you! Keep on trusting the One who has called you.

* * * * *

On Sunday morning, June 30, 2019, I stepped up to the podium centered in the sanctuary of North Olmsted Evangelical Friends Church. As had been suggested by pastor Geoff Schultz one year earlier, arrangements were made for me to share my testimony with the church congregation. At the same time, I would also have the opportunity to announce that my book, *At Last I Open My Heart*, had recently been published.

With a microphone in hand, I cordially greeted the men and women seated in the church auditorium. "For those of you who may not know me," I started, "my name's Bart Mercurio, and I've been a member here at Friends Church for the past four years. It's indeed an honor for me to have this opportunity to speak to you this morning on Mission Sunday."

"Back in December of 2016," I continued, "an event called *Hallelujah, God Is Near—a Patchwork of Christmas* took place right here at our church. Some of you may recall that wonderful evening. It was a glorious celebration of fellowship and worship. That same evening, I also gave a testimony about my lifelong struggle with addiction. This morning, I'm here to tell you more about that struggle, introduce you to a book that was recently published, and share with you why I believe God is calling me to carry out a special mission."

As I spoke, my book's colorful cover, an illustration of a man triumphantly standing atop a mountain peak with outstretched arms while gazing upward toward a heavenly setting of blue skies and snow-white clouds, was brightly illuminated onto a wide, overhead screen suspended from the ceiling above the sanctuary.

"My book, *At Last I Open My Heart*," I resumed, "begins during the early years of my childhood and takes the reader through a seventy-year journey that ends on a Sunday morning in 2015 when, in fact, I was standing exactly where I'm standing now, receiving a special blessing from our senior pastor as he warmly welcomed me as a new member of Friends Church. Those moments, which I recreated in the final pages of the book, are very special to me.

"*At Last I Open My Heart*, which I wrote from a biblical perspective, is a powerful testimony about forgiveness, repentance, and redemption. It's a straightforward and honest story, and I believe that it sends a powerful and inspirational message."

I paused briefly, randomly making eye contact with several members of the congregation seated in pews that were divided by two wide aisles, each one leading to a main entrance at the rear of the auditorium.

"Looking back," I began, "I can tell you that I once led an extremely immoral life. I lived in my own hidden world until a November morning in 2001 when I was shamefully exposed of my secret life. Bluntly put, I was a man addicted to pornography for more than forty years, and I deeply regret the disgraceful things that I did during those years."

"I did not honor or respect God," I confessed. "I cursed him again and again, questioning why he would ever create a man as worthless and evil as myself. I was angry and bitter for a very long time, yet God never abandoned me. He never gave up hope for me. He never stopped loving me. All along, he had a plan, and that plan was to uncover the fallen soul of a spiritually dead man."

I cast my eyes downward for an instant, then humbly lifted my head upward, briefly capturing the mixed expressions of a handful of men and women seated throughout the auditorium.

"I would not be standing up here this morning," I continued, "if not for the amazing grace of God because you see, that same God, who I fought for most of my life, created me in his image and not the image of a worthless, evil man given over to a life of lies, deceit, and immorality. From the very first moment of my conception, God had a purpose and a plan for my life. He had a purpose and a plan for a man who believed himself to be totally worthless, a man who thought that his entire life was a failure."

As I spoke, I fought back tears. "God forgave me, and in spite of the unspeakable sins that I committed throughout my life, my heart was transformed and my soul was redeemed. I repented. I sought the professional help that I so desperately needed to turn my life around to recover from my immoral lifestyle before it was too late. For five years, I met weekly with a dedicated, Christian counselor, and with his help, I came to understand the causes, motivations, and irrational thoughts that triggered my self-destructive, harmful behavior."

I then referred to an Old Testament passage, comparing the content of the verses to my own life. "In Genesis 50:20, we see the evil plotted against Joseph by his brothers, but we also see God turning that same evil into good. I pray that God will do the same in my own life, using the message of my book to turn evil into good among the lives of those who are struggling as I once did."

"I lived through the nightmare of pornography," I stated harshly. "I know firsthand the damage and consequences that it causes. It led to the dissolution of two marriages and it crippled me financially for years."

Raising my voice, I then joyfully proclaimed the good news. "But by the grace of God, I recovered from a dreadful addiction, and this morning I stand here before you to celebrate a great victory over it!"

Applause resounded throughout the auditorium, affirming the congregation's joint acknowledgment of my triumph over evil.

"I will challenge this widespread epidemic," I promised, "an epidemic that devastates millions of lives around the world every day—both secular and Christian alike. I will challenge this awful, flourishing industry that continues to ravage and corrupt innocent souls, destroys the God-given sanctity of marriage, and tragically feeds human sex trafficking across the globe."

"No one," I asserted, then repeated with emphasis, "*no one* should ever be led to believe that pornography is harmless. It can seduce any man or woman in the blink of an eye.

"The story I began writing eleven years ago is now a book, and I consider myself blessed by its publication. I believe with all my heart—a heart that was once closed to the outside world for half a century—that God is now calling me to move forward with a special mission to minister to those who struggle with pornography. I will honor and serve God as I am now ready to share my story of redemption whenever and wherever it needs to be heard."

Pausing once again, I then set aside a couple of minutes to humbly acknowledge my pastor's key role in the success of my book. "Before closing, I wish to also give a special thanks to our senior pastor. From the first moment that I mentioned to Pastor Geoff that I was writing a book and for the years that followed, he has always been there to encourage and support me. I now wish to personally thank him, not only for his exceptional service as our senior pastor but also for his role as a genuine friend. From my heart, Geoff, I thank you, because without your ongoing support and encouragement, I do not believe that I would be standing up here this morning."

I concluded my presentation by announcing that a table had been provided for me in the nearby family life center. "You're invited to stop by and visit me," I said. "Copies of my book are available, and I'll be glad to answer any questions you may have. Please keep me in prayer, and I thank you very much for the opportunity to share my testimony with you this morning."

I stepped away from the podium, then made my way through a nearby hallway to the family life center. Church members soon gathered by the book's poster display table, which had been set up earlier that morning. For an hour or so, I met with men and women who openly discussed their difficulties and struggles with addiction issues. I listened carefully and offered feedback and encouragement during our conversations. My hope was that *At Last I Open My Heart*, which revealed the true story of my miraculous recovery from decades of addiction, would provide inspiration and comfort to others.

I silently thought back to the analogy of Genesis 50:20 that I had briefly discussed during my presentation. Even though Joseph's brothers intended to harm him with the evil plan that they devised, the resulting evil eventually led to good. Though I was in no way proud of the immoral life that I once lived, I sincerely believed that the words from the Genesis passage could also allow evil to turn to good in the lives of those who were struggling as I once did.

When I arrived home later that afternoon, I was surprised to discover an anonymous, incoming message on my cell phone. It was received from someone who attended the Sunday morning service and had listened to my testimony. I immediately read the text, which contained these words: "I didn't get a chance to catch up with you at church, but I did want to tell you that you did a fabulous job speaking this morning. You articulated well! Thank you so much for sharing! And God bless you! I was very moved!"

Tears gathered in my eyes as I read the enlightening text message for the second time. I was very moved by the message. The words not only encouraged me but reinforced my belief that God was definitely calling me to embark on a very special mission. My published book would serve as a stepping stone and pillar of hope for others.

I revisited the words in Genesis 50:20: "You intended to harm me, but God intended it for good to accomplish what is now being done, the saving of many lives." That verse reassured me that the evil of my past was meant for future good. I vowed to honor and serve the Lord, and I prayed that I would be armed with the tools needed to successfully share my testimony with others so that they, too, could pursue a path that would enable them to also celebrate a great victory over addiction.

4

A Perfect Storm

For our struggle is not against flesh and blood, but against the rulers, against the authorities, against the powers of this dark world, and against the spiritual forces of evil in the heavenly realms.

—Ephesians 5:3

During the pandemic years of 2020 through 2022, much has been written about COVID-19 and its far-reaching impact on the global, pornography industry. In "Coronavirus & Lockdown Impact on Porn Industry," Inventiva, a world leader in digital marketing, shares that pornography is not only a global, multibillion industry but also that at least forty million Americans admit to visiting related websites on a regular basis.[13] These numbers are alarming. Vulnerable men and women have sadly fallen prey to the evils of pornography. War must be declared against this debilitating scourge that daily devastates millions of innocent souls throughout the world.

In August 2020, "What You Need to Know about the Pandemic and Porn" appeared on First Things First, a website founded by an organization established in 1997 with a primary goal of providing research-based resources to assist in enabling people to not only discover the joy of healthy relationships but also to seek the strengthening of those relationships as well. The article's informative study affirms the disastrous effects generated by the pornography industry throughout the recent pandemic:

> 2020 might be the year everyone wants to escape from and/or forget for so many reasons. This means we shouldn't be surprised to learn that many of us are looking for ways to escape the pain and fear. One of the escapes that has seen a dramatic increase in use during the coronavirus pandemic is pornography. A variety of sources report a 16% to 30% increase in use in the United States since March.[14]
>
> To give you some perspective, consider these two statistics: Every second, 28,258 users are viewing porn, and approximately $3,075.64 is spent on pornography each second on the Internet. Let those numbers sink in for a second. Those are staggering, to say the least.[15]
>
> In *Psychology Today*, Dr. Justin Lehmiller, an American social psychologist and author, explains that the coronavirus pandemic virus is not just affecting the amount and type of pornography being produced. It's also affecting how much people are consuming and what they're searching for on major sites. According to Dr. Lehmiller, during one month's time there were more than nine million searches for coronavirus-related pornography, such as people wearing masks, surgical gloves, or gowns while engaging in sex. He explains that these searches are, in part, triggered by the fact that people are at home with much more time on their hands than usual. But he and other experts say there are other potential reasons for increased porn site visits. Some of those reasons include using sex as a coping mechanism for dealing with fear of disease and death, or loneli-

ness, or a dramatic increase in experiencing anxiety, stress, or negative emotions.[16]

Most people don't realize how pornography reaches out and grabs them. Research shows that when a person sees pornography, the brain releases endorphins, secreted hormones that are hundreds of times more potent than morphine and more addictive than cocaine. These hormones, also secreted within the nervous system, gives one an enormous false sense of well-being(https:fightthenewdrug.org/). A nonprofit and nonlegislative, anti-pornography organization founded in Utah and active since 2009, Fightthenewdrug.org likens pornography to eating junk food. It seems like it is really good and that it satisfies you for the moment; however, it actually leaves you wanting more and more and never feeling full.[17]

Additionally, research consistently indicates that pornography use can hurt a couple's relationship. This is especially true when one person is frequently viewing pornographic images online. In their discussion of dangers of porn (htttps:// Gottman.com/blog/an-open-letter-on-porn), Drs. Julie and John Gottman argue that intimacy for couples is a source of connection and communication between two people, but when one person becomes accustomed to constantly getting pleasure from pornography, he or she is actually turning away from intimate interaction. When watching porn, the user is in total control of the sexual experience, which is in contrast to normal sex in which people are sharing control. Moreover, pornography can lead to a decrease in relationship trust and a higher likelihood of affairs outside the relationship.[18]

As a result of the coronavirus pandemic and of people having been quarantined, many have commented on how they didn't realize how much they really need in-person, face-to-face experiences for their emotional well-being. The research is clear: while a person may be using pornography as a coping mechanism, the thirst for it is insatiable. And it still leaves them feeling empty, unfulfilled, and needing more.[19]

In its introduction, "What You Need to Know about the Pandemic and Porn," First Things First demonstrates how one of the most common escapes from the pain and fear of COVID-19 is the use of pornography, which increased dramatically during the pandemic years.

As human beings, we are innately equipped to search for pleasure. Seeking too much pleasure can become extremely harmful. I learned that firsthand during the many years in which I continued to constantly resort to pornography as a regular source of pleasure. Achieving that pleasure provides a thrilling sense of gratification, but when that intoxicating and exhilarating feeling of gratification becomes a personal one and becomes steeped solely in the satisfaction of one's own sexual urges, then serious, long-term harm is bound to unravel.

Kristine I. Batcho, PhD, a licensed psychologist and professor at Le Moyne College in Syracuse, New York, discusses the pursuit of pleasure in "Too Much Pleasure, Not Enough Happiness":

> Do you find yourself seeking more and more pleasurable experiences, big and small? Our culture encourages the pursuit of pleasure.
>
> So many entertainment venues are readily available, and marketing can seduce people to try new products and activities to expand their options. Sports, fitness gyms, concerts, and online gaming are examples of just a few of the

myriad of opportunities for enjoyment. But do all these pleasures add up to happiness?[20]

Feeling good isn't the same thing as being happy. With pleasure, we can reach an optimal level; beyond which what we enjoy can become boring or worse. Some people can become obsessed and seem to never have enough. Many things are harmless, but others, like drugs or alcohol, can gain control over a person. Rather than leading to happiness, an addiction can then be physically, emotionally, and socially devastating.[21]

Imagine a life focused on pleasure without regard for others. Can pleasure be as sweet when indulged in alone as when shared with others? Unlike physical things, pleasure expands as it is shared. If seeking pleasure hurts others or damages relationships, joy is diminished and interpersonal losses are suffered. In retrospect, social costs might be understood as too high of a price to have paid for those pleasures. In an ironic cycle, an excessive drive for pleasure can lead to isolation and loneliness. Loneliness then fuels the pursuit of pleasure to compensate for lost social support.[22]

* * * * *

My history of indulging in Internet pornography escalated considerably during the months leading up to the morning of November 1, 2001, the date on which my long, secret addiction was initially exposed. While Diana, then my wife, was at work away from our home, I squandered hour after hour with my eyes riveted to the monitor of a personal computer. During a period of several weeks while I was unemployed, I often found myself home alone and unable to resist the temptation of surfing the Internet and accessing one obscene website after another. I eventually became so immersed in my immoral activity that the very thought of even being red-hand-edly discovered rarely phased me.

On weekday mornings, I'd routinely tell Diana that I loved her, then smile, and wave to her while she backed out of our driveway to leave for her nearby workplace. Disregarding the hypocrisy of my deceptive behavior, I'd allow about ten minutes to pass, believing that would be sufficient time for Diana to arrive at her workplace. A short time later, my eyes were intently glued to a computer screen as I steadily enjoyed one lewd image after another, obscene images that continued to flash before me. Lustfully craving more and more of those graphic images, minutes would soon turn into hours. During that dark period of my life, pornography evolved into my greatest love. It drove me into deep denial, and I hopelessly struggled with my obsession while engulfed in a secret, self-serving world that disconnected me from a loving and faithful wife.

I'm very ashamed of the immoral behavior that I once practiced, and I have often questioned how I could have repeatedly deceived my wife, expressing love for her while at the same time betraying her trust by secretly lusting after thousands of obscene images. How was it that I would not recognize my harmful and hypocritical behavior and why would I willfully and flagrantly destroy the very intimacy that was reserved for the sanctity of marriage?

I became sexually addicted long before the COVID-19 pandemic started its surge across the globe during the early months of 2020. My first exposure that specifically involved Internet pornography was in late 1999 when I one day randomly accessed a pornographic website on a desktop computer at my workplace. During the weeks that ensued, though I vainly attempted to avoid unblocked, objectionable websites, I far too often failed. I did not resist the recurring temptation to view obscene images even though I was fully aware that should my disrespectable pornography habit be discovered by my employer, my position as regional operations manager would severely be jeopardized. Though the tremendous risk of losing my job loomed daily, I nevertheless continued to pursue the uncontrollable and irresistible urges that constantly triggered my patterns of immoral behavior.

By late summer of 2001, a few weeks after I had been furloughed from my position—ironically, not because of pornography use but because my employer had reorganized and downsized the company operations—my addictive behavior took a turn for the worse. During several weeks of unemployment, while I often remained alone at home, I conveniently took advantage of the available opportunity to excessively indulge in unlimited and undisturbed sexual pleasure. There is little doubt that my selfish indulgence contributed heavily to the destruction of my marriage. Though Diana and I later worked together in a diligent attempt to repair our marriage during the four-year recovery period that followed my exposure to addiction, full restoration of her trust always remained an uphill battle. Betraying Diana with my secrecy and dishonesty severely breached her trust, which produced an indelible stain that was virtually impossible to ever completely remove from our marital relationship.

In her book, *Reclaim Your Life—You and the Alcoholic/Addict*, author and clinical psychologist, Carole Bennett, MA, discusses the dangers of boredom:

> As the saying goes: An idle brain is the devil's workshop. People with too much time on their hands may find themselves in hot, troubled, waters. People who tend to be bored may also be weary or restless due to a lack of personal interest or motivation. They are bored with themselves, their jobs, and their life.[23]
>
> Boredom usually stems from a state of complacency, void of challenges or creativity. Everyone gets bored now and then, but it is important to acknowledge the difference between changing that mood through healthy alternatives versus, for instance, sitting around with friends to share a few high-flying hits. That kind of reaction to boredom can ultimately lead to an antisocial, unhealthy path toward addiction.[24]

> Boredom takes some perseverance to shake off. It is a state of mind and it requires committed determination to do something about it or change up the routine. People can form a habit of being bored, especially if no one expects anything from them, and in turn, they don't expect anything from themselves. Drugs or alcohol can seem like acceptable choices to alleviate the routine of boredom. It only takes the easiest, quickest fix—requiring little or no effort to get high or drunk and *poof*…you're not bored anymore![25]

Though her work as a clinical psychologist and counselor revolves heavily around the treatment and recovery of individuals who struggle with alcohol and drug addiction, I believe that Carole Bennett would be likely to agree that the pornography habit with which I battled for many decades is yet another, unquestionable, destructive pattern of behavior that is easily triggered by unfortunate spells of idleness.

* * * * *

The *Merriam-Webster* dictionary describes a "perfect storm" as a critical or disastrous situation created by a powerful concurrence of factors. It is often used as an analogy for an unusually severe storm that results from a rare combination of meteorological events.

Journalist and Author Sebastian Junger published his book, *The Perfect Storm*, in 1997. The success of the book brought about the phrase "the perfect storm" into popular culture. The term's popularity was accelerated with the release of a 2000 feature film adaptation of the book. After the release of the motion picture, the phrase gradually grew to signify an event where a situation is aggravated drastically by an exceptionally rare combination of circumstances.[26]

The COVID-19 pandemic arrived suddenly and unexpectedly in the United States in late January 2020. Over a period of several months following the onset of its arrival, millions of men and women found themselves experiencing unwelcome feelings of lone-liness and fear. Frequent lockdowns throughout America, mandated by the rampant spread of the virus, spawned isolation, idleness, and boredom. As a result, searching for a pleasurable experience, which is often inherent to our nature, became quite ideal and created a warmly received remedy to serve as a consummate substitute during a turbulent time wrought with hopelessness and despair.

Instant access to a personal computer or a mobile device pro-vides an immediate opportunity to search for pornography during any twenty-four-hour time frame. The coronavirus pandemic, com-bined with an unusual set of factors and circumstances, effectually created a situation similar to "a perfect storm," conveniently setting the stage for individuals to seek pleasure rather than sulk in loneliness or fear. Though viewing pornography undeniably is likely to produce a pleasurable experience, a tremendous risk exists in surrendering to addictive patterns of behavior. Ultimately, such addictions invariably trigger not only harmful but drastic consequences as well.

Luke Gibbons is the director of marketing for Kingdom Works Studios based in Stuart, Florida. *The Conquer Series*, which he discov-ered and first released in 2014, is a powerful, cinematic small group study video series that has helped more than one million men dis-cover freedom from pornography. In 2019, *Charisma News*, a website magazine that presents its content to a Christian audience from a spiritual perspective, included "The Destructive Force That Enslaves a Large Portion of the Church,"[27] an article in which much of the shared information focuses on Luke Gibbons, who himself struggled for several years prior to successfully recovering from addiction:

> Luke Gibbons grew up in a Christian home, but he says, "I grew up and found pornography online and it just got deeper and deeper for me. It really took me into a spiraling addiction that lasted ten years, right from when I was in high school, then to university, then to working full-time. Sometimes I'd be up all night viewing and then go to work on an hour's sleep. I knew that

God didn't want me in that space." Gibbons also knew he had to get help. He had tried to overcome his pornography addiction on his own, but until he opened up to men who had the same struggles, he remain trapped in the bondage that had gripped him for so many years.

Through his transparency, Gibbons discovered *The Conquer Series,* a video program that has helped more than one million men—including Gibbons—in eighty countries around the world, to walk in freedom from this destructive force. The series fulfills the words of James 5:16, which tells us to "confess our sins to one another that we may be healed." *The Conquer Series* research reveals that a staggering number of churchgoing men view pornography on a regular basis. And many churchgoing women, teens, and even children also secretly struggle with viewing pornography. The secrecy in itself exacerbates the problem.

"If we have pain in our life, we can medicate it through pornography without anybody knowing it," says Gibbons, head of marketing and church relations for Kingdom Works, producer of *The Conquer Series.* "But at the core," he continues, "we know about it, and that eats away at us. Until we get help, it's going to continue to do that."

Luke Gibbons' story demonstrates that no one is immune from the vise-like grip of pornography. Another of his articles, "15 Statistics About the Church and Pornography That Will Blow Your Mind," affirms the widespread severity of pornography:

Statistics reveal that the rapid spread of pornography cannot be ignored. But it is not a problem affecting just men. Women, teenagers, and children are also being caught up in it at alarming rates. Many assume that the church is immune. They see the smiling faces of the people who attend church and might be thinking, "certainly, such godly folks could not be viewing pornography." But many reports have come out over the last several years that show quite a disturbing picture. Not only has pornography invaded churches, but in many cases, statistics show that Christians—and even church pastors—engage in viewing it at almost the same rates as the secular population.[28]

Research studies, primarily by the Barna Group and Covenant Eyes, reveal that initial exposure to pornography generally begins in childhood and then progresses. Access to it is increasingly easy due to the Internet and other wide variety of formats that are available, such as printed materials, DVDs, television, and much more. The following data allows us to see the scope and effects of pornography in society as well as the church.

There are around forty-two million pornography websites, which total around three hundred seventy million pages of content. Pornography use increases the marital infidelity rate by more than 300%. The average age of a child first exposed to pornography is eleven. 87% of Christian women have watched pornography. More than 50% of pastors not only view pornography on a regular basis but also agree that addiction to it is by far the most damaging issue in their congregation.[29]

So what should we do? These statistics can be overwhelming. The fact that pornography has such a tight grip on our society does not mean the church is helpless to fight against it. Instead, Christian leaders must stand up and lead their churches through the battle. First, leaders must be willing to admit that the problem exists in their churches. You can't treat a disease until you know it's there. You must realize that pornography is a disease and that it's steadily growing within the church body.[30]

I believe that the COVID-19 pandemic effectively created "a perfect storm." Unless that storm is quelched and calmed, millions will continue to be lured into the destructive web of evil that pornography breeds. Lives will be destroyed. Marriages will crumble. Souls will be lost forever. The awful tragedy of human trafficking will escalate into an even much more deplorable, worldwide problem.

We must stand strong against this horrible monster. We must unite against this reprehensible scourge of mankind. This multibillion-dollar industry that wreaks havoc throughout the world must be infiltrated, rooted out, and driven to its knees.

The words in Ephesians 6:10–13 serve as a mighty battle call:

> Finally, be strong in the Lord and his mighty power. Put on the full armor of God so that you can take your stand against the devil's schemes. For our struggle is not against flesh and blood, but against rulers, against authorities, against powers of this dark world, and against spiritual forces of evil in the heavenly realms. Therefore, put on the full armor of God, so that when the day of evil comes, you may be able to stand your ground, and after you have done everything you can, you will continue to stand.

Beyond this perfect storm that has risen during one of the greatest pandemics of our time, we must boldly join hands to battle a formidable enemy. Let us do all within our power to serve the Lord and pray together to conquer this evil force that daily devastates the lives of millions of men, women, and children around the world as Ephesians encourages us, the time is now to put on the full armor of God and to take our courageous stand.

We must be motivated by the great message in Romans 8:31: "What, then, shall we say in response to these things? If God is for us, who can be against us?"

5

For Such a Time as This

And God said, "Let there be light," and there
was light. God saw that the light was good, and
he separated the light from the darkness.

—Genesis 1:3–5

On June 5, 2019, at age seventy-five, I was delighted to learn that I had become a published author when *At Last I Open My Heart*, an autobiographical account of my struggle with addiction, was nationally released. Since its publication, the book has served as an inspirational tool for many readers and has scored a great victory over pornography, a catastrophic addiction that impurifies countless souls throughout the world. As a former addict who battled this disgraceful addiction for decades, I have experienced firsthand the tremendous damage that can ultimately prevail. The reckless and constant use of pornography not only inevitably led to the dissolution of two marriages but also crushed me financially along the way. While leading an extremely immoral life in the secrecy of my own hidden world, I transformed into an empty, lonely, lost soul, hopelessly adrift in a world of darkness for nearly half a century.

Having successfully recovered from my addictive behavior, I now stand firm in my belief that hope always remains for others to escape from the painful bondage that I once experienced. After my long, harrowing experience, I consider myself equipped to do combat with a foreboding enemy that once tried to completely destroy my life. I am now prepared to reach out and help those who continue to struggle as I once did. No man or woman is completely free from the icy, steely, deadly grip of pornography. It is a monstrosity that became even more rampant during the unexpected invasion of the COVID-19 virus that struck America during the early months of 2020. We must no longer simply ignore this menacing force of evil.

The book of Esther in the Old Testament contains the elements of a great novel. It is a story about a beautiful woman called by God to save her nation of Israel. We follow the life of Esther, a young, Jewish orphan girl as she rises from obscurity to eventually become a queen. Living in a foreign nation, she is elevated to a position of royalty which enables her to save her people from mass genocide. The historical events occur during the reign of King Xerxes (486–465 BC) in the Persian empire.

Though the phrase, "for such a time as this," appears only once in the book of Esther, the words parallel a time in which we live during the twenty-first century. I believe that it is at such a crucial time as this that we, as Christians, must courageously stand together to decimate the forces of evil that continue to drive us deeper into the darkness of the world with each passing day.

Dr. Tony Evans, senior pastor of Oak Cliff Bible Fellowship in Dallas, Texas, writes:

> Esther was to risk her life and her legacy with no guarantees of a positive outcome. That's the "for such a time as this" Mordecai challenged Esther to accept—"and who knows if you have not attained royalty for such a time as this? (Esther 4:14)[31]

Dr. Evans moves forward with his discussion:

> And that's also the "for such a time as this" God sets before you and me. God has given each

of us a job, position, resources, education, and more. God has opened opportunities to optimize His kingdom purposes. He didn't place you or me where we are so we could post pictures on social media all day long. He placed us wherever we are because we are in the midst of a battle, a war. You and I are in the midst of a seismic conflict involving good versus evil.[32]

To miss a kingdom assignment because we've become too caught up in our personal kingdom is one of the greatest tragedies we could ever face. An entire nation was grateful for how Esther responded to Mordecai's rebuke. Their lives were spared. How many souls can be spared in the culture where we live today if we choose to step up to service, even if it involves sacrifice?[33]

In a practical application of Esther 4:13–14, the Enduring Word Bible Commentary explains that God promotes us and puts us in a place for a special reason and that we need the courage and wisdom to perceive that reason and to continue to walk in it.[34]

In today's culture, I believe that the pestilence of pornography has erupted in "such a time as this." Though our country—and the entire world as well—have been stricken by the deadliest pandemic in more than one hundred years, pornography has infected the earth for much, much longer. It, unfortunately, arrived long before the surge of the COVID-19 virus. Tragically, its use has escalated exponentially during recent decades. Internet pornography has exploded into out of control proportions, aided significantly by easy public access to the World Wide Web, which sprouted into millions of homes and workplaces during the late 1990s.

Pornographers everywhere have seized all convenient opportunities to continually take advantage of technological advances to enhance their production and distribution of visual pornographic images. Subsequently, people throughout the world have been deceived and tempted into viewing more and more obscene content.

Perhaps one of the saddest consequences of all is that revenues from the pornography industry have risen dramatically to billions and billions of dollars.

In recent years, many helpful books from both Christian and secular perspectives have been written regarding the dangers of pornography. Although several authors are men, a respectable number of women have also successfully tackled this taboo topic. Many others, including pastors, have themselves been former addicts and have experienced the devastating consequences that pornography addiction caused in their own lives. Clinical psychologists have also made noteworthy contributions, especially by providing informative and educational online information that has proven helpful to those who are willing to step out of denial of their addictive behavior and follow through with the subsequent steps necessary to move forward toward a successful recovery.

More sermons in our churches should be presented to affirm the extensive harm that results from the abusive use of pornography, a topic that is far too often soft-pedaled as one of little significance. Winning the war against this overpowering and dreadful enemy will be extremely challenging and very difficult. Millions of people, myself included, are former addicts who were once blindly ensnared by its dreadful lure. Communities must valiantly join together in a no holds barred attempt and unite to eliminate this terrible scourge.

Pornography should not be condoned by anyone. Sadly, it is not likely to disappear from the face of the earth too soon. We must label it as the deadly poison that it truly is. Men and women everywhere should be trained to fully recognize its adverse consequences. We must practice these virtuous words: Finally, brothers and sisters, whatever is true, whatever is noble, whatever is right, whatever is pure, whatever is lovely, whatever is admirable—if anything is excellent or praiseworthy—think about such things (Philippians 4:8).

* * * * *

D. Scott Hildreth is the director of the Center for Great Commission Studies and Assistant Professor of Global Studies at

Southeastern Baptist Theological Seminary in Wake Forest, North Carolina. A missions and evangelism professor, one of his most valuable accomplishments is *Bondage and Freedom: Escaping the Trap of Pornography*.[35] He stated that his real goal in writing the book was to give some tips and keys on how to escape pornography and how the gospel may also actually help to free one from the grips of pornography. The book is directed to a wide audience, both Christian and non-Christian, including his own young students, both male and female, who have struggled with pornography addiction at one time or another.

In "4 Effective Ways to Escape the Grip of Pornography," Professor Hildreth bluntly summarizes the goal of pornography:

> You see, the truth of the matter is this. Pornography is a multibillion-dollar industry that has one goal: to hook you, to hold you, and to take everything you have to wreck your life and to ruin it. It's worse than a casino that takes all the clocks and all the windows out and doesn't let you know what time it is. The goal of pornography is to prey on the most basic human nature—your sexuality, your temptations, your lusts—the way that God created you.[36]

He continues,

> I'm with guys all the time who say, "God, would you please just take away the desire?" And I say, "God will not answer that prayer." If God answered that prayer, the human race would cease to exist. So God can't answer that prayer, "God, take this desire from me." But what God does do is give us the Holy Spirit of whom one attribute is self-control. God gives us the ability to control ourselves as we strive to escape pornography.[37]

According to Professor Hildreth, one of the major steps in escaping from pornography is to realize its destructiveness:

> Realize the power and the negative influence that pornography will have upon you. It's not a simple, little step of sin. You see, it does something on the inside of you, not just on the outside. It rewires your brain. It reshapes your body. We need to take the pornography temptation and really put the face of destruction and disaster on it, rather than the cuteness or the attractiveness of it.[38]

Pathways Real Life Recovery, founded in 2007, is an addiction treatment center located in Sandy, Utah. Its website states that people struggling with addictions often think, *I am not deserving. I am not lovable. I am worthless. I can't.* In addition, the stigma, fear, and desperation associated with addiction often weigh you down, and you might not know where to turn, what to expect, or what questions to ask. The good news for those who struggle with addiction is that none of those thoughts are really true.[39]

In "Steps to Overcome Pornography Addiction," which appears on Pathways Real Life Recovery website, several vital issues are discussed concerning the nature of the addiction:

> At a certain point, pornography viewing ceases to be merely a bad habit and becomes an obsessive-compulsive addiction. Those caught in this cycle can recognize the stages in their pornography viewing habits. From the initial sexual thoughts, a feeling of fear and a desire to avoid watching are triggered; despite these feelings, the compulsion to watch pornography becomes too great, leading to a sense of shame and guilt after watching. While a person trapped in this cycle will vow to never watch pornography again, sex-

ual thoughts recur and lead to yet another round of the same pattern.[40]

The first step in overcoming an addiction to pornography is recognizing what healthy sexuality looks like. For those with a beneficial sexual outlook, their sexual expression is positive and enriching as they both give and receive while experiencing pleasure. This type of sexuality benefits the individual emotionally and spiritually as well as physically. In contrast, an unhealthy sexuality involves a sense of shame around sexual thoughts, a feeling that one's sexual energy is uncontrollable or a desire to use sex to exploit others through power or force or in a way that is not consensual. In general, pornography addicts have this sexual outlook as they use pornography in order to feel wanted, important, or powerful.[41]

In "Steps to Overcome Pornography Addiction," Pathways Real Life Recovery not only advises how to recognize the signs of pornography addiction but also how to treat the underlying causes as well:

Common signs of an addiction to pornography include increasing social isolation, defensiveness or guilt regarding your pornography usage, continued reliance on pornography despite the negative consequences, a loss of control and inability to stop, obsessive thoughts about pornography, and/or a strain in your relationship and intimacy with your partner. Understanding and addressing the underlying causes that are contributing to your pornography addiction is an important step on the road to recovery. For many people, pornography or excessive Internet use in general become methods to use to self-soothe in response to depression, anxiety, stress, trauma, boredom or loneliness. Addressing these under-lying causes can make overcoming the addiction much easier.[42]

In "The Pornography Trap," the late Dr. Victor Cline, a for-mer emeritus professor of psychology at the University of Utah and a clinical psychologist credited with extensive experience in coun-seling men who suffered from pornography addiction, named four critical stages of pornography that follow its initial exposure: *addiction*; *escalation*; *desensitization*; and *acting out*. *Addiction* is the desire and need to keep coming back for pornographic images. It starts as entertainment but then becomes an obsession. *Escalation* describes the stage where pornographic users become bored and soon need more explicit, brutal, and decadent images to produce sexual plea-sure. *Desensitization* arises because practices once viewed as shocking or taboo are soon seen as acceptable or commonplace, and *acting out* is the tendency to perform the behaviors that one has viewed, which may include exhibitionism, sadism, masochism, group sex, rape, or other deviations.[43]

The second stage of *escalation* is discussed in greater detail by Dr. Cline:

> Following *desensitization*, the problem usu-ally escalates. In order to get their highs, kicks, and erotic turn-ons, those addicted to pornogra-phy develop a desire for more aberrant materials.
>
> One man explained "If I saw something gross yesterday, I need to find something more gross today. If I see something deviant today, I must look for something more deviant tomorrow. Another young man said, "After a few months of viewing pornography, I found myself less and less satisfied with the soft stuff. I wanted pictures that were more graphic and more extreme. It's like taking a drug that loses its effectiveness over

time. Soon you have to take more and more just to get the same feeling you used to get with less."

The Internet makes such graphic portrayals accessible and affordable, and anonymous—those three A words combine to feed the escalation and create an almost insurmountable challenge for those trying to escape the trap of pornography.[44]

Throughout the pages of my first book, *At Last I Open My Heart*, I disclosed behavior in my own life that specifically exemplified the escalating levels of my addiction:

> I started patronizing adult bookstores on a regular basis, and when the magazines and the paperbacks failed to satisfy my hunger for pornography, I indulged in another thrill—viewing peepshows in the bleak shadows of video arcades. Yet even the peepshows couldn't quench my gluttonous, lustful urges. I had to go further. I had to go deeper. And before long, I found myself drawn into a dark, forbidden world—the world of voyeurism. I took foolish risks to seek uninhibited pleasure, flagrantly ignoring the grave consequences that might result because of my disgraceful, criminal behavior.[45]
>
> My addictive activity was often unmanageable. Again and again, I tried to unconscionably satisfy my boundless thirst for lust. I hopelessly drove myself deeper and deeper into the immoral world of pornography, powerless to abandon my prurient pursuit of sexual desires. At some stage during the late 1960s, I closed my troubled heart to the real world. I did not rediscover or reopen that closed heart until the start of the next century.[46]

I ascended the ladder. When I reached the top step, I surveyed the shadowy area beneath the roof of the building. It consisted primarily of dust-covered, steel beams and wire hangers that supported lighting fixtures and plasterboard ceiling tiles. I guessed that my targeted area would be situated somewhere beneath that section, which was no more than ten feet away from where I stood. Hearing voices rising from below, I excitedly, yet cautiously, walked across a long, sturdy beam while anxiously anticipating how I would soon secretly enjoy peaking through any one of the narrow openings between the suspended ceiling tiles.[47]

These past situations represent explicit depictions of how my obsession with pornography grew deeper and deeper, often culminating at a point that rendered me powerless to overcome uncontrollable urges that triggered me into more and more risky activities, some even bordering on the edge of criminal behavior.

* * * * *

Pure Life Ministries, based in Dry Ridge, Kentucky, is a pioneer in the treatment of sexual addiction and its consequences. For more than thirty-five years, thousands of people have discovered freedom through its counseling programs and teaching materials. As a guest author, Tom Blangiardo, a former business executive and entrepreneur, who started serving as Outreach Director for Pure Life Ministries in 2003, shared his own gripping story on Pure Life's website in 2019. His powerful testimony is discussed in "The Poison of Pornography." Like millions of other men, myself included, he witnessed firsthand the destructive consequences of pornography:

My first exposure to pornography came as a defenseless child, less than ten years old. I innocently rode my two-wheeler down to the neighborhood candy store where I always spent my weekly allowance, and there it was. It was in the early years of *Playboy* magazine leading the way for a whole new genre of "adult entertainment," and the magazine was prominently positioned. Something went into me that day that I could not shake. I came back a day later and rifled through the pages, filled with both shame and overwhelming excitement. The images were indelibly planted in my mind. Like Adam and Eve, a whole new world had opened up to me. Little did I know that I had been bitten by a vicious serpent, and its deadly venom had entered my soul.

Although the poison is not deadly in one dose, the serpent is relentless. By his repeated and progressive attacks, the serpent's victim becomes increasingly unable to resist. Satan is a patient predator. He studies and understands his victim. He doesn't present his corrupted view of reality all at once, but rather step by step, lie by lie, as he sees the target ready to accept the next dose. Through my early adult years, pornography became a regular part of my life, progressively drawing me deeper into magazines, adult movies, strip clubs, you name it. I was raised in a church-going family but that did nothing to abate my habit. Satan had convinced me that these practices were just a harmless way to satisfy a single man's natural desires. After all, he assured me, it's a "victimless" crime…it hurts no one. "Have fun, be merry, for tomorrow you may die," became my mantra.

By the time I married at age thirty-two, pornography was firmly entrenched in my heart and had completely distorted my views of women, sex and marriage. I thought I loved my wife, but the truth was, I entered marriage overcome by a "what's in it for me" attitude. It says in Genesis 3:1 that *"the serpent was more cunning than any beast of the field,"* and sure enough, Satan's lies took a new turn on his now-married prey. It did not take much for him to persuade me to enrich and add excitement to our sex life. My new wife was hesitant but acquiesced to my pressure. The excitement lasted for a while, but soon our relationship began to unravel as I expected her to do and be what my pornographic inside-world had convinced me was the way to a happy and fulfilling *love* life. It did not take long for her to harden and pull back, feeling used and unloved in many ways that went far beyond the bedroom. The fact was the world of pornography that Satan had led me to had utterly destroyed my capacity to love my wife. We were divorced in four short years.

I married again, five years later. The result was the same. Unaware and disillusioned of what I had become, I then also fell prey to the most sinister of all of Satan's lies, self-pity. He assured me, "You deserve better than this. God has let you down." Over and over again, this message convinced me that I had a right to indulge in my sexual sin.

The serpent now went in for the kill. The stronghold in my heart that I had yielded to him, this harmless and "victimless" pornography led me down roads I never thought I would travel as I yielded to sexual sin of all kinds. Sex became medication to me, but a drug whose potency became less and less effective, as I needed more and more to dull the pain of what I had become in my life. Weekends would go by where I would spend $ 5,000 or more on my sin and end up deeper in depression and despair. Any hope I once held of lasting joy and happiness, or even a normal life, had evaporated.

Satan's poison of lies and false promises had disabled me, leaving me in a spiritual and emotional trance that took complete control over my life. I had lost touch with reality, with Truth. I had become literally insane. It was clear that the ultimate victim of pornography was me, and that I had forfeited all the promises that could have been mine in Christ. Until Jesus intervened.

I know now why He had to allow me to go so far, to go down so many dark alleys, and for so long. I was finally backed into a corner, desperate and totally out of options when He extended His hand to me, *"Come to me, all you who labor and are heavy laden, and I will give you rest."* (Matthew 11:28)

His offer was to come into the Pure Life Ministries Residential Program where He would reveal Himself, and correct the lies about myself, about life, and about Him. It was at Pure Life Ministries that He opened His word and gave me hope. Though once living in a cesspool of pornographic images and imaginations, my mind is now clear and free. I am married now eight years and learning to love a woman sacrificially and unconditionally. All that I had lost has been restored, and so much more.[48]

* * * * *

Marripedia, a joint project of Marriage and Religion Research Institute and International Organization for the Family, is an online social science encyclopedia that specializes in matters related to family, marriage, religion, and sexuality. It synthesizes the work of social science into concise, specific topics to inform and educate its readers.

One of the entries that appears on the *Marripedia* website is "Effects of Pornography."[49] This topic specifically describes a wide range of devastating consequences that will generally result from pornography addiction. An insightful discussion follows:

Pornography changes the habits of the mind and the inner private self. Its use can easily become habitual, which in turn leads to desensitization, boredom, distorted views of reality, and an objectification of women. There are also numerous clinical consequences to pornography use, including increased risk for significant physical and mental health problems and a greater likelihood of committing a sex-based crime.

The "digital revolution" has led to great strides in productivity, communication, and other desirable ends, but pornographers also have harnessed its power for their profit. The cost has been a further weakening of the nation's citizens and families, a development that should be of grave concern to all. The social sciences demonstrate the appropriateness of this concern.

Two reports, one by the American Psychological Association on hyper-sexualized girls, and the other by the National Campaign to Prevent Teen Pregnancy[50] on the pornographic content of phone texting among teenagers, make clear that the digital revolution is being used by younger and younger children to dismantle the barriers that channel sexuality into family life.

Pornography, as a visual (mis)representation of sexuality, distorts an individual's concept of sexual relations by objectifying them, which, in turn, alters both sexual attitudes and behavior. It is a major threat to marriage, to family, to children, and to individual happiness.

Social scientists, clinical psychologists, and biologists have begun to clarify some of the social and psychological effects of pornography, and neurologists are beginning to delineate the biological mechanisms through which pornography produces its powerful effects on people. Its ability to undermine individual and social functioning is powerful and deep. Its effects are on the mind, the body, and the heart.

Regarding its effect on the mind, pornography significantly distorts attitudes and perceptions about the nature of sexual intercourse. Men who habitually look at pornography have a higher tolerance for abnormal sexual behaviors, sexual aggression, promiscuity, and even rape. In addition, men begin to view women as "sex objects," commodities or instruments for their pleasure, not as persons with their own inherent dignity.

Concerning its effect on the body, pornography is very addictive. The addictive aspect has a biological substrate with dopamine hormone release acting as one of the mechanisms for forming the transmission pathway to pleasure centers of the brain. Also, the increased sexual permissiveness engendered by pornography increases the risk of contracting a sexually transmitted disease or of being an unwitting parent in an out-of-wedlock pregnancy.

As for its effect on the heart, pornography affects people's emotional lives. Married men who are involved in pornography feel less satisfied with their marital sexual relations and less emotionally attached to their wives. Women married to men with a pornography addiction report feelings of betrayal, mistrust, and anger. Pornographic use may lead to infidelity and even divorce. Adolescents who view pornography often feel shame, diminished self-confidence, and sexual uncertainty.

The *Marripedia* topic, "Effects of Pornography," is an exceptional resource that straightforwardly informs and warns us of the numerous, ill-fated effects that may result from pornography use. Even more alarming, pornography has been sadly identified as a gateway to human sex trafficking, perhaps one of the most criminal tragedies that has ever emerged in our world.

In "How Pornography is Linked to Human Trafficking," Luke Gibbons writes this in his blog on the *Charisma News* website:

> To most people, sex trafficking is a problem that exists in distant, foreign countries. You may think, "But it certainly isn't something that would involve me, is it?" But if you view pornography, then the answer is yes. The truth is that pornography and sex trafficking have strong links, even in the United States, where the sex trafficking industry is three billion dollars a year.[51]
>
> How big is the sex trafficking problem? The University of New England reports it is the third largest criminal business in the world, trailing only drugs and weapons. On April 11, 2018, the White House defined sex trafficking as a global form of modern-day slavery in which individuals are coerced to perform commercial sex acts against their will. Their report also alarmingly added that according to the International Labor Organization, nearly five million victims were

forced into sexual exploitation and that of these, over 99% of the trafficked individuals were women and over 21% were children.[52]

Luke Gibbons continues to explain how pornography is connected to human sex trafficking:

> According to journalist, John-Henry Westen, "As long as America's men are being trained to think that violent, disturbing pornography is sexually acceptable, an enormous clientele for sex traffickers is created every day in homes, college dorms, and apartments across the nation."
>
> The Trafficking Victims Protection Act defines sex trafficking as "the recruitment by any provision or obtaining of a person for the purpose of a commercial sex act." It also includes "inducing commercial sex acts by force, fraud, or coercion." A "commercial sex act" is "any sex act in which anything of value is given or received by any person." Since performers are given money and other items of value, the definition certainly applies to the pornography industry.[53]
>
> But are performers coerced or induced by force or fraud? Aren't all the scenes performed by consenting adults? One former porn actress testified, "Women are lured in, coerced and forced to do sex acts they never agreed to do…and even given drugs or alcohol to help get them through hardcore scenes…the porn industry is modern-day slavery." Sex traffickers use pornography in many ways. They force their victims to watch porn to desensitize them, even to train them in sex acts they will be forced to perform. They also video the victims and sell and distribute the

pornographic films on the Internet and other outlets.[54]

"How Pornography Is Linked to Human Trafficking" includes other very important opinions as well:

> Noel Bouché, executive director of pure-HOPE, explains, "While pornographic content includes trafficked victims from around the world, porn consumers aren't told anything about the performers, including which ones may have been trafficked from an early age. Regular users of Internet pornography are likely to be consuming pornography that includes adult and child victims of sex trafficking."[55]

On Redeeming Love's blog, Katie Tomkiewicz provides us with this stark summary:

> Various studies show that when pornographic content is viewed, the viewer's mind becomes increasingly calloused to the brutalities of the sex-trafficking industry, which include rape, coercion, sexual violence, and the general idea that women are objects existing for the purpose of providing sexual pleasure. The psychological effects that pornography has on the mind cannot be denied; the harm done to both the viewer and the viewed cannot be denied. It is critical to address today's pornographic culture for what it is: a hub for sex trafficking and a gateway drug for future traffickers.[56]

The Exodus Road is an international organization that fights human trafficking in many foreign countries throughout the world. Its headquarters are in Colorado Springs, Colorado, and it was founded in 2012 by Matt and Laura Parker after a two-year period of research in which they partnered with police to investigate hundreds of bars and brothels throughout southeast Asia to learn as much about human trafficking as possible. Their overall vision is to see a world in which human beings are never bought, sold, or exploited. Their mission is to disrupt the darkness of modern-day slavery by partnering with law enforcement to fight human trafficking crime while equipping communities to protect the vulnerable and empowering survivors as they walk into freedom. [57]

In "Porn and Human Trafficking: The Facts You Need to Know," an article that appears on The Exodus Road website, we learn much more about the global impact of the tragedy that has been identified as human sex trafficking:

> When it comes to sex trafficking, many people know that it can happen in the prostitution industry. But how are pornography and human trafficking related? Sex trafficking hides in brothels and hotels, where "johns" (people who pay for sex) can purchase time with a trafficked individual to exploit them. But there are other forms of sex trafficking outside of forced prostitution. The commercial sex industry is diverse. Human trafficking occurs in each sector, especially within the pornography industry.[58]

> The United Nations Office on Drugs and Crime defines human trafficking as any situation in which "force, coercion, abduction, fraud, deception, abuse of power or vulnerability, or giving payments or benefits to a person in control" are used to exploit another person. In the pornography industry, human trafficking takes multiple forms. Unfortunately, because of the way pornography is produced and distributed, trafficking can be hard to identify.[59]

The Exodus Road article also describes what trafficking looks like in the pornography industry:

> Trafficked individuals are often exploited in more than one way. Some traffickers take explicit photos of victims as a means of control, threatening to shame them by exposing the photos to their families. Traffickers then sell the content by uploading it to porn sites while simultaneously exploiting the victims through prostitution. In other cases, survivors have been exploited solely for the purpose of producing pornography.[60]

Included in the same article is a response to this question: What about pornography content on free websites?

> Free accounts do not mean that no one is profiting. Approximately 90% of free porn websites and nearly 100% of pay porn websites buy their material from an outside source. If traffickers upload exploitive content of trafficked individuals for free, website owners still profit from the traffic generated. This is where the line between legal pornography and human trafficking becomes blurry. Several of the world's most popular porn websites have been found to host legal content alongside illegal content. Some websites' profits can amount to millions each year from illegal and abusive content.[61]

The Exodus Road international organization should be commended for its dedicated work in seeking justice for human sex trafficking. It has assisted police in both finding and freeing survivors of human trafficking as well as in arresting traffickers for legal prosecutions. In Exodus Road's own words, "For the sake of the many survivors still enduring abuse and who deserve freedom, every rescue and every arrest matters."

Fight the New Drug, an anti-pornography organization founded in 2009, soberly reminds us that "One person trafficked is one too many." According to the organization, which is based in Utah, there is no easy call to action to end sex trafficking:

> Tackling that industry would need the full help of governments all over the world to enforce laws and to protect the vulnerable, just to get started. How do you kill an industry? Well, if no one wants to buy a product, then it just doesn't sell. Stopping the demand for sex trafficking starts with each one of us. If you hate the idea of sex trafficking, if it is shocking and horrible to you, then consider what millions of people visually consume around the world every day.[62]

"God's children are not for sale"—that is the takeaway message from *Sound of Freedom*,[63] a motion picture about the true story of a homeland security agent, Tim Ballard, who risked his life to save many young children who were victims of the Colombian sex trafficking trade. The movie is not only a true and powerful account of the tragic realities of human sex trafficking but also a courageous, groundbreaking story that encourages everyone to assist in decimating the horrible scourge of human trafficking that exists in our present-day world.

Every year since 2010, the United States President has dedicated January as National Slavery and Human Trafficking Prevention Month. On its website, the US Department of State provides a fact sheet about the awareness of different forms of human trafficking domestically and abroad through United States embassies and consulates. Also celebrated are the efforts of anti-trafficking organizations, communities of faith, state and local law enforcement, survivor advocates, businesses, and private citizens all around the world to promote this very important cause. The department reminds us that everyone can play a vital part in ending human trafficking in the United States and around the world.

* * * * *

The phrase, "for such a time as this," appropriately comes to mind in "Sexual Counter-Revolution,"[64] written by Scott Yenor, a professor of political science at Boise State University and a Washington Fellow at Claremont Institute's Center for the American Way of Life. He passionately discusses the demoralization of our nation in the wake of an ongoing sexual revolution. The opening sentences of his article immediately capture our attention with these stirring words:

> Flyers were recently distributed at Stewart Middle School in Tacoma, Washington, that targeted eleven-year-olds, informing them that they could have sex with anyone under the age of thirteen, and that their parents were not entitled to determine whether they took birth control or were tested for sexually transmitted diseases. The kids could make up their own minds. Flyers and sex-ed programs are leading edges of a revolution that has been gaining power over the West's moral imagination for more than two generations. Liberals, feminists, and gay activists press it forward.
>
> Dishonest catchphrases of "choice" and "freedom" are used to promote the revolution. But when it comes to marriage, sex, family, and sex roles, the notion that choice governs is always an illusion. Every society has a sexual constitution. With the tools of honor and shame, the sexual constitution shapes desire, guiding it toward certain experiences and expressions and away from others. It teaches citizens what it means to be a man and what it means to be a

woman. It determines the rank of marriage, sex, and child-rearing among the goods that people pursue.

Two ideologies shape the reigning sexual constitution: feminism and sexual liberation. Feminist ideologues seek a world "beyond gender" in Judith Butler's words. This means formulating laws and enforcing taboos so that differences between men and women evaporate and socialization toward distinct gender roles is prohibited. Feminists seek a society in which women achieve emotional and economic independence from domestic duties and family life. In the pursuit of female independence, sexual taboos that encourage enduring and monogamous marriage are themselves made taboo.

Sexual liberationists want a society "beyond repression." Boundaries must give way to enlightened expressive sexuality until "repression" vanishes and people are free to pursue sex as they wish. Love is love. New taboos stigmatize as "haters" those who perpetuate traditional sexual mores.

New obstacles arrive as progressive mores are adopted. Effort is redoubled. Eleven-year olds must be taught to question their identities. Four-year olds must sit on the laps of gay men dressed as sexualized women, who read picture books to them. Strictures against adult sex with children must be "problematized" and eventually overcome. Monogamy is ridiculed, called oppressive, and replaced with polyamory. The revolution keeps on rolling, "beyond gender" and "beyond repression," toward the abolition of marriage and marital norms.

The author straightforwardly continues:

> Conservatives and family activists have been standing athwart the sexual revolution shouting "nature" for decades—to little effect. Nature imposes limits, but not in the way conservatives hope. True, males and females act and think differently from one another under our new sexual constitution, in a rebuke to the androgynous hopes of feminists. A supermajority continue to desire the old-fashioned discipline of monogamy and marriage, in a rebuke to sexual liberationism. But the persistence of nature does not portend a return to norms supporting marriage and family life. Instead we get a new man and a new woman, shaped by our new constitution. Neither is suited for marriage and family life as they existed under the old constitution.
>
> We cannot depend on nature alone. Our new sexual constitution remakes sexual desire and intimate relations, reshapes the sexes, builds new institutions, and leads to a new hierarchy of human goods. Like a command-and-control economy, our re-engineered ways of being male and female work poorly. Liberalized sexual mores disrupt the male-female dance. Stable marriage becomes a luxury good. Family life frays. Both intimate relations and domestic life become dysfunctional.

Scott Yenor concludes his treatise by suggesting that the sole alternative to the sexual revolution is counterrevolution:

> The rolling revolution has overturned every aspect of gender roles, marriage, and family that our great-grandparents took for granted. It seems

unstoppable. But this is to misjudge history. The sexual revolution was born in the imaginations of those who raged against what they perceived as inhumane moral prohibitions and stultifying social expectations. Now that their revolution has remade our world, we can see that it ruthlessly reorders female socialization to accord with the desires of elite women, leaves men poorly formed, undermines marital stability, damages children, disorients young people with the promotion of homosexuality, and immiserated men and women alike. A counterrevolution must destroy this new constitution. The cause is righteous and our indignation is just.

* * * * *

We are reminded in Ecclesiastes 3:2–8 that there is a time in our world for everything:

> There is a time for everything and a season
>   for every activity under the heavens:
>   a time to be born and a time to die,
>   a time to plant and a time to uproot,
>   a time to kill and a time to heal,
>   a time to tear down and a time to build,
>   a time to weep and a time to laugh,
>   a time to mourn and a time to dance,
>   a time to scatter stones and a time to gather them,
> a time to embrace and a time to refrain from embracing,
>   a time to search and a time to give up,
>   a time to keep and a time to throw away,
>   a time to tear and a time to mend,
>   a time to be silent and a time to speak,
>   a time to love and a time to hate,
>   a time for war and a time for peace.

In such a time as this, it is a time for war against pornography. The light must pour into the darkness to purge this deadly enemy. We must wholeheartedly attempt to band together to obliterate not only the crippling addiction to pornography but the irreverent horrors of human sex trafficking as well.

From the book of Esther, Mordecai's words ring loud and true: "And who knows that but you have come to your royal position for "such a time as this?" We must remain faithful to the inherent meaning of the words spoken to Esther. It is in "such a time as this" that the darkness and evil of our fallen world must be infiltrated by the illumination of the light that God has provided.

6

A Woman: Not an Object

This is the verdict: Light has come into the world, but
people loved darkness instead of light because their
deeds were evil. Everyone who does evil hates the
light and will not come into the light for fear
that their deeds will be exposed.

—John 3:19–20

During her remarkable career, Audrey Hepburn, listed by the American Film Institute as one of the greatest female screen legends during the Golden Age of Hollywood,[65] was among the most beautiful and talented actresses throughout the 1950s and 1960s. When asked to reveal the secrets of her beauty, the poised, glamorous actress responded with these enduring words:

> The beauty of a woman is not in the clothes
> she wears, the figure that she carries, or the way
> she combs her hair. The beauty of a woman is
> seen in her eyes, because that is the doorway to
> her heart, the place where love resides. The true
> beauty of a woman is reflected in her soul. It is
> the caring that she lovingly gives, the passion that

she expresses. And the beauty of a woman only grows over the years.[66]

Audrey Hepburn's words epitomize beauty in its own right. In "Why Audrey Hepburn Will Always be More Than Just a 'Pretty Face,'" Journalist, Sanjana Ray, takes care to describe the legendary actress with complimentary and inspirational words:

> She was the beacon of effortless grace, natural elegance, and implausible beauty. But those aren't the reasons why she was everything I wanted to be when growing up. It was because she was a beautifully, purposely determined, and boundlessly kind human being.[67]

The late Audrey Hepburn was undeniably a beautiful woman, and like all other women, she was not created to live in this world simply as an object—especially a sex object. No woman created by God was born into this world to serve solely as a sex object. Throughout history—past, present, and future –females have been, are, and will remain beautiful creations of God. Their primary purpose on this earth has never been to serve in a specific provocative role as a sex object. Wives are not sex objects. Nor are mothers or daughters. The objectification of women is a tragic problem in today's world. *Wikipedia* provides sobering information about the adverse ramifications that sexual objectification often causes with regard to a woman's health:

> Some feminists and psychologists argue that sexual objectification can lead to negative effects including eating disorders, depression, and sexual dysfunction, and also can give women negative self-images because of the belief that their intelligence and competence are currently not being, nor will ever be, acknowledged by society. Sexual objectification of women has also been found to

negatively affect women's performance, confidence, and level of position in the workplace.[68]

The general consensus is quite apparent. Sexual objectification offers no benefit for any woman. It is an enormous challenge for any female, adult or teen, to avoid the pitfalls commonly associated with this critical issue.

During my years of addiction, the use of pornography undeniably and unquestionably involved the sexual objectification of women. My uncontrollable, immoral behavior thrived on the objectification of women. Not until God presented me with a door of opportunity to step out of denial and seek redemption did I discover the key that unlocked a heart that had been secretly hidden for decades. Not until then did I realize that a woman should never be solely looked upon as a sex object, plaything, or toy. Not until then did I truly understand that a woman is a beautiful creation of God.

* * * * *

In his article, "And God Created Woman," Author Geoffrey Thomas, who served as pastor of Alfred Place Baptist Church in Wales from 1965–2015, uses Genesis 2:21–22 to demonstrate the differences between men and women:

> There are males and females because that is the way God designed the human race. We are told in Genesis 1:27, "So God created man in his own image, in the image of God he created him; male and female he created them." Both male and female were created by God and they share equally in God's image, but they are different. One of the differences is the fact that they were made in different ways, Adam being created from dust while Eve was made from Adam.[69]

In elaborating on the uniqueness of Eve's creation and why she was purposefully created from Adam, the author provides this explanation:

> Because God made woman from man, Adam immediately recognized that she was something of himself. "*This is now bone of my bones and flesh of my flesh,*" said Adam. She was of Adam and from Adam. She was made of the very same substance as himself. She wasn't made out of inferior stuff, nor was she made of superior stuff. She was the very bone of his bone and flesh of his flesh. God chose to build her from Adam's *rib*—the word is used everywhere else in the Bible as the *side* of something. Here alone in the English Scriptures, it is translated "rib." There are some beautiful familiar comments on this fact that go back to an ancient Jewish commentary on the Torah and then were later picked up by the puritan, Matthew Henry, in his own commentary, which I will quote because of their truthfulness: "Eve was not taken from Adam's head that she should rule over him, nor from his feet, to be trampled under foot, but she was taken from his *side* that she might be his equal, from under his arm that she might be protected by him, near his heart, that he might cherish and love her."[70]

In the closing paragraphs of "And God Created Woman," we are shown that the creation of Eve resulted in Adam's rejoicing:

> Adam neither said anything ego-reinforcing nor anything degrading to Eve. Adam just needed one look and in his unfallen state he saw that only God's glorious sense of beauty and creative power could have brought to him so perfect

a partner. The woman-sized void in his life that no other creature could satisfy was filled. I'm sure that Adam would have taken the language of the Song of Songs if he could have known it and said to the woman, *"How beautiful you are, my darling! Oh, how beautiful! Your eyes behind your veil are doves…All beautiful you are, my darling; there is no flaw in you"* (Song 4:1, 7).

When God created Eve, the first woman, he certainly did not create her to serve exclusively as a sex object, especially to appease the lustful desires of just any man. No woman was created to be degraded or demeaned or treated as a sex toy to simply satisfy a pleasurable means to an end. Women were created for a very special purpose to be cherished and loved by men.

* * * * *

Millions of young men, including myself, discovered great pleasure within the pages and centerfolds of the men's magazines that became readily available during the 1950s. Soft-core material was predominant at that time and provided most of the titillating content in the earlier issues of men's magazines. Total circulation of a few of the magazines grew rapidly and accounted for millions of subscribers by the 1960s; magazines included much more sexually explicit content by then. Some even dared to combine urban lifestyles with pornographic-oriented pictorials. By the 1970s, newer magazines took their content a step further by depicting hardcore themes that were much more provocative than their predecessors.

Viewing centerfolds or other uncensored photos was naturally irresistible to men, especially young men—not only irresistible but extremely impressionable as well. Many of the alluring images that were first captured in magazines were not routinely erased from one's memory. Those first images of viewing pleasure easily became the foundations that significantly impacted the future use of pornography.

My own early exposure to hardcore pornography occurred in 1962. At the time, I was enrolled as a freshman at Ohio State University. I describe those early, impressionable moments in detail in my first book, *At Last I Open My Heart.*

> On a late autumn evening, shortly after I started attending Ohio State University, I overheard raucous laughter from an adjacent dormitory room. Quite curious about the commotion, I soon found myself surrounded by a half dozen men who were gathered together. They seemed to be engrossed with the content of a deck of playing cards. I wondered how an ordinary deck of cards provided such an unusual source of excitement and entertainment. Minutes later, I had my answer as I stared at the face of one of the cards. I was not only shocked, but mesmerized by the scene that appeared before me. I had never viewed such an obscene depiction of a group of men and women sexually engaged with one another. I became more astounded when I viewed yet another scene on the face of a second card, this one more visually licentious than the first.[71]

Scenes such as the ones that I viewed more than sixty years ago remained embedded in my mind for decades to come. Once exposed to explicit sexual images, they are not easily removed from your memory. An attempt to simply reprogram your brain so that such images magically disappear and never resurface again is nearly impossible. That is how powerful the lure of pornography can be. You remain vulnerable indefinitely and at any unexpected moment may be suddenly attacked by random, recurrent, obscene images.

Avoiding temptation is quite difficult and as soon as you surrender to it, matters will most likely become progressively worse. During the course of my long struggle with pornography, I must have surrendered to temptation thousands of times, unwilling to accept the fact that I was not likely to escape from my patterns of addictive behavior before first stepping out of denial and realizing the true extent of the harm that I caused myself.

Over and over again, I viewed most women as sex objects, often irrationally justifying my thoughts and actions by aggravated inner feelings of self-pity. Totally convinced that most women hated me and viewed me as a worthless man. I adamantly believed that I was far too evil to ever be admired or truly loved by a woman. Because of my self-deprecating attitude and my misguided perceptions, I indulged myself deeper and deeper into immorality.

Females were simply playthings and sex objects available to secretly fulfill pleasure during my dark, twisted fantasies. Only after forty years of addiction was I finally exposed to my secret life. Only then did I gather up enough courage to step out of the darkness and into the light. Only then did I finally realize the truth that God did not create women for me to selfishly exploit as my own personal sex objects.

In the early stages of my addictive cycle, I attained sexual satisfaction by browsing through, then purchasing a variety of explicit magazines that were always readily available for sale in any one of several adult bookstores in surrounding communities. It was not uncommon for me to squander away hours thumbing through hundreds of photographs of nude women, provocatively posing either alone or in groups. Those images fed my unrestrained appetite for lust.

Never totally satisfied, I indulged myself even further by viewing X-rated videos that would more widely appeal to my lustful desires. I also viewed obscene peep shows behind the drawn curtains of private booths in dark arcades of adult bookstore basements. Always craving more, I searched for darker material, finally reaching a point where I was willing to take huge risks to seek greater thrills. I struck bottom when I shamefully explored an obsession with voyeurism. I simply shrugged off my borderline criminal behavior while seeking to disgracefully and recklessly engage in detestable patterns of immoral activities. Only by the grace of God, my out-of-control addiction was exposed before it was too late before I might justifiably become a hardened criminal or, worse yet, a dead man.

As I think back to the immoral lifestyle that I secretly practiced, I am overcome by deep shame. I was once a lost man who hardheartedly misconceived the true beauty of women by abusively objectifying them. I failed to realize the truth that God had not created women to serve as sex objects. I inexcusably exploited the true essence of a woman's beauty in exchange for selfish, prurient purposes. Tears fill my eyes when I recall how I once blatantly and callously objectified so many unknown females. Would any of those nameless women ever forgive a man for such undignified, disreputable behavior? At this stage of my life, I often pray with all my heart that God has protected the lives of all the unknowing women who I once secretly and scandalously targeted as sex objects.

During the four years of counseling that I underwent while recovering from my addiction, I came to appreciate the significance and the true beauty of a woman. I, at last, began to realize that without exception, each and every woman who was objectified during those dark years was not only a beautiful creation of God but also someone's precious mother or daughter who had not been created to serve solely and abusively as my sex object.

* * * * *

Not yet eight years old, I learned that I was suffering from very poor eyesight. Excerpts from *At Last I Open My Heart* demonstrate the extent to which I dreaded wearing thick eyeglasses:

> The pair of dark-framed eyeglasses hooked snugly around my ears. The thickness of the glasses embarrassed me so much that I soon withdrew from most of my classmates. Very ashamed and overcome with shyness, I often hid my bespectacled face between the covers of a textbook. By my early teen years, my thick glasses plagued me to the point that I started experiencing border-

line signs of paranoia. Whenever I heard nearby laughter, I immediately cringed, concluding that others were mocking me because of my unsightly appearance. I hated viewing my reflection in a mirror. My glasses became a personal crown of thorns and caused me to frequently struggle with feelings of self-consciousness and inferiority.[72]

Until I started wearing contact lenses two years after I graduated from high school, my greatest fear was rejection. I viewed myself as an unsightly monster and regularly wondered whether a female would even consider dating me.

While I was in my senior year at Maple Heights High School, I recall one Friday evening when I removed my thick eyeglasses to gather up enough courage to ask a classmate if she would dance with me. Jan was a very popular, attractive cheerleader who had been crowned homecoming queen of the senior class. Infatuated by her beautiful smile and upbeat personality, I developed a head-over-heels secret crush, viewing her as an enchanting young goddess. Though I believed it would be impossible, I often fantasized about how great it would be if I were her steady boyfriend, but that was a wishful fantasy that I ruled out to be impossible. After all, I often reminded myself, why would one of the most popular girls in the senior class want to be seen with a guy as unsightly as me?

On an October evening in 1960 at a sock hop dance that followed a sporting event, I decided that despite how much I hated my thick eyeglasses, I would wait no longer. I removed my glasses, blurring my vision considerably, then awkwardly made my way across the gymnasium floor toward Jan, who was mingling with a few of her friends. As I approached her, the dreadful fear of rejection was rushing through me. I softly greeted her, then bravely asked if she would like to dance. When she smiled and said yes, I was awestricken and delighted. For an instant, I believed that a miracle had been performed and that I had been suddenly transported to paradise. The joy and relief that streamed through me was indescribable. Those were among the greatest moments of my young life. The very thought of slow dancing with Jan, my secret crush, propelled me to the top of the world. I drifted into heavenly bliss as we started to dance.

While we danced, I wondered if I had enough courage to ask Jan for a date. I quickly dismissed that notion, convincing myself that I would surely be rejected. If she refused, the rejection would be far too much to bear. So I instead seized the moment, and as I warmly wrapped my arm around her waist, we quietly danced in the center of the high school gym. Basking in an elevated state of euphoria, I slow danced with Jan for the next few minutes. I still remember the song that was playing during those moments. It was "The Way You Look Tonight,"[73] a popular song performed by the Lettermen. Here are the opening words to the romantic ballad:

> Someday, when I'm awfully low,
> When the world is cold
> I will feel a glow just thinking of you
> And the way you look tonight

I always smile when I think back to how special those moments were for me on that long ago Friday evening as I danced with the attractive cheerleader who was my secret high school crush. I also smile when I think back to another Friday evening in October 2011 when I attended the fiftieth reunion of my senior class. Though Jan and I hadn't seen one another during all those years, warm memories resurfaced and I decided that I finally had an opportunity to reveal my secret crush.

I greeted her about halfway through the evening. "Jan"—I smiled—"it's great to see you. I hope you're doing well."

"I am," she replied, smiling back.

We spoke briefly, only for a few minutes, about the same amount of time that we danced together fifty years earlier.

She seemed a bit intrigued when I said, "There's something I must tell you, Jan."

I paused for a few seconds, then confessed, "I want you to know that there was a guy in our class who wore thick glasses and had an incredible secret crush on you."

She flashed that same smile that was just as beautiful then as it was in high school. She then startled me with these words, "Wow! Really? I wish I would have known that."

We laughed together, then cordially parted ways. Her response surprised me. Had I overlooked a golden opportunity all those years ago? Recalling the bittersweet memory, I thought to myself, *Bart, you're fifty years too late.*

I wanted to share this memory about Jan because throughout my life, I often viewed myself as a failure. Jan's response was a true eye opener that led me to ponder about all the *maybes* that might have been. Maybe, Jan would have dated me after all. Maybe, it really didn't matter that I wore such thick eyeglasses. Maybe, Jan would have admired me for who I really was and how I really felt. And who knows? Maybe she would have even fallen in love with me.

I once sadly thought that I would never be loved by a woman. I have made countless unwise decisions during my life and while I was addicted to an immoral lifestyle that often bordered on Jekyll and Hyde syndrome behavior, I wandered down a narrow, self-destructive path for a very long time. Saddest of all, I targeted women as sex objects for many years. I secretly controlled and manipulated them in my own universe—a false world where I continuously dwelled on my own dark fantasies. My greatest battle was with my own conscience. Though I was aware of the difference between rightness and wrongness, I chose to disregard the truth and remained in deep denial for many years.

Thinking back to my senior year in high school, I did not view Jan as an object, especially a sex object who would merely satisfy my lustful desires. I was simply a teenage guy who developed a secret crush on a teenage girl who happened to be a popular cheerleader. I admired her beauty, her personality, and her radiant smile. My great wish was that Jan could have been my steady girlfriend and I could just hold her hand and feel that someone really loved me and cared about me. I needed a hand to hold and someone to love me.

There have been several key women in my life. I rarely viewed them as sex objects. Not Louise, my first wife, or Diana, my second wife, or Brenda, to whom I had been engaged during the early

1980s, or to Nina, a very special woman who loved me passionately. I share each of their stories in much more detail in *At Last I Open My Heart*.[74] They all expressed their love for me, but my heart was closed for far too long. Though I desperately yearned for love, I believed that I was unworthy to receive it.

I have learned to appreciate the beauty and vulnerability of a woman. Throughout the years, many motion pictures containing memorable scenes have moved me deeply. One such scene appears in a 1999 romantic comedy, *Notting Hill*.[75] Toward the end of the movie, Anna Scott, a beautiful and very successful world-renowned actress, is standing in front of William Thacker, a not-so-successful business owner of a Notting Hill bookstore. Anna will soon be leaving the country, but she decides to first stop by the bookstore to bid farewell to the man with whom she had briefly shared a romance which had suddenly ended. In an unforgettably endearing scene, a vulnerable, successful, actress humbly opens up her heart with these words: "After all, I'm just a girl standing in front of a boy, asking him to love her." That is a very powerful scene that moves me deeply. It personifies not only the vulnerability of a woman but the power and beauty of love itself.

Another similar motion picture scene is set during the closing moments of *Fireproof*,[76] a 2008 drama about a fire department captain, Caleb Holt, and his wife, Catherine, whose marriage is in deep crisis. Caleb has not only become somewhat selfish but addicted to internet pornography as well. Unable to tolerate his behavior, Catherine decides to divorce him. He becomes determined to renew his faith and break his pornography habit and sincerely tries to reconcile his marriage to Catherine. She eventually realizes how much he truly cares about her. Their differences are resolved and the marriage is saved. Catherine wishes to share her heart and unexpectedly appears at Caleb's fire station and asks to see him. He is surprised to see her and while they are standing several feet apart from each other, she humbly expresses herself with these touching words: "If I haven't told you that you're a good man, you are." If I haven't told you that I've forgiven you, I have, and if I haven't told you I love you, I do."

A third memorable motion picture scene that draws a deeply emotional response appears during the closing moments of the 1940 epic film *City for Conquest*.[77] As the movie opens, a flashback in the streets of New York City introduces us to two preadolescent children who are the main characters in the story. Danny Kelly seems destined to become a great boxer, and his girlfriend, Peggy Nash, is a gifted dancer who dreams to one day be a star. Fast forward to a scene twenty years later, and we see Danny and Peggy attending a dance party. Though the two are planning to be married, Peggy decides to achieve her lifelong dream when she is swayed by a local dance champion to become his professional partner.

When Peggy tells Danny that she is not ready to marry, he becomes embittered, and they irrevocably part ways. Not long afterward, Peggy's new dance partner is not only attempting to control her life but also trying to sexually abuse her. Meanwhile, Danny has risen through the ranks as a boxer and earns a chance to fight for the world title. During the championship bout, he is deliberately blinded by his opponent who cheats by repeatedly striking him with rosin dusted gloves.

A few more years pass, Peggy's career as a big-time dancer is shattered, and she is reduced to dancing at seedy New York nightclubs. Danny's boxing career has ended because of his severely damaged eyesight, and he now works at a local newsstand. Toward the end of the film, Peggy, learning about Danny's fate, unexpectedly appears at the newsstand one evening. She still believes that he is very angry at her for leaving him years earlier. Danny senses her presence and struggles with his poor vision to capture a glimpse of her. As she softly greets him by name and asks how he is doing, she suddenly bursts into tears.

Danny tells her that he is doing fine and tries to comfort her. Tenderly smiling, he affectionately tells her, "I can see you okay, Peg, and I always knew that someday you'd pass by here because no matter what, I knew you'd always be my girl."

As they warmly embrace, Peggy responds, "Always, Danny, always." It is an emotionally packed ending as we empathize about a man and a woman who, despite their past trials, profess undying love for one another.

The scenes described in the closing moments of *Notting Hill*, *Fireproof*, and *City for Conquest* clearly demonstrate the everlasting power of genuine love between a man and a woman. Anna Scott, Catherine Holt, and Peggy Nash, though fictional female characters, embody the vulnerability and beauty of women created in God's image. Genuine love between a man and a woman should always be enduring and very special.

7

Love Makes the World Go Round

Many waters cannot quench love;
rivers cannot sweep it away.

—Song of Solomon 8:7

According to Justin Lehmiller, PhD, a social psychologist and research fellow at Kinsey Institute, lust is a state of overwhelming and physical attraction to another person. "Love, on the other hand," he states, "is a much broader concept that includes deeper emotional connection and generally a desire to make that relationship last." Lust is predominantly a sexual and physical connection while love is predominantly a romantic, emotional, mental, and a spiritual connection.[78]

In *At Last I Open My Heart,* I describe in my own words the hurt and frustration that I experienced as I struggled to discover genuine love throughout the greater part of my life:

> I thought that I was in love with a woman who would never abandon me, but I was mistaken. I felt rejected because I failed yet again. Brenda's words certainly rang true. I was not only a hypocrite. I was worthless as well. And how could a worthless man ever be loved?[79]

Fighting back tears, I stepped back into my apartment and slowly sat down on my sofa. My mind drifted, thinking first about Louise, the tall, slender woman with reddish-brown hair who fifteen years earlier had instantly fallen in love with me. We seemed so happy as husband and wife until our six-year marriage simply unraveled. Louise was unwilling to consider reconciliation and our young family was swiftly uprooted by the ugliness of divorce.[80]

I next turned my thoughts to Nina and my effort to rebound from a failed marriage. I fell deeply in love with Nina, a stunning, breathtaking woman with dark brown eyes and long, frosted hair. I envisioned a life of eternal bliss with her forever by my side. Our story, however, was little more than a fairy tale. I naively believed that our relationship would go on forever, but instead it suddenly ended after she sadly became involved with the use of drugs. My unanticipated breakup with Nina severely broke my heart and I grieved over her lost love for more than two years.[81]

And just now, Brenda, my young fiancée, with cascading, dark brown hair and sky-crystal, blue eyes, had unexpectedly decided to immediately end our long engagement. Though a wedding date was only two months away, she made it clear that she was no longer interested in our relationship and that she wished to simply step away from my life. Our lengthy romance had been so promising and I honestly believed that I would at last share a lifetime of love with a woman who truly cared about me.[82]

A profound sense of emptiness swept through me as I solemnly realized that I failed drastically with each relationship—Louise, Nina, and Brenda. I seriously wondered whether I could ever inseparably share an everlasting, loving relationship with one special woman. As I basked in self-pity during those disconsolate moments of hopelessness and uncertainty, I felt extremely lonely and unwanted. All I really wished was that I could know and somehow believe that there was one woman somewhere who would always love me. I just wished that one special woman would hold my hand and assure me that she would always love me. I desperately wanted to believe that I was a special man and not a worthless one.[83]

* * * * *

Burdened by a troubled heart that was hidden away from the real world for more than forty years of my life, I indulged in a self-serving, secret lifestyle that drove me into an inescapable web of lust. During those distressing years, I relentlessly searched for a woman who would genuinely love me.

Following the dissolution of my first marriage in 1974, I wandered about aimlessly, quite insecure much of the time. I numbed my mental and emotional pain by patronizing local bars where I regularly picked up women, single or married, several times a week. While hungering for a woman to love me, I often found myself involved in one-night stands. Enjoying a few hours of raw, sexual pleasure during one adulterous affair after another did not serve as a substitute for genuine love. After each promiscuous encounter, I felt lonelier and lonelier. I was searching for genuine love in the wrong way and in all the wrong places.

By the autumn of 1983, I had become a lost, lonely soul, steaming with unmitigated lust and knee-deep in a twenty-year history of sexual addiction. The heavy baggage that I carried with me cultivated ill feelings of self-hatred and unworthiness. Though I dreaded the secret lifestyle in which I wallowed, I was incapable of gathering up sufficient courage to abandon my unhealthy patterns of immoral behavior. Overwhelmed by recurring, negative thoughts, I viewed myself as an evil, despicable man who did not deserve to be loved. Although I yearned to meet a woman who would truly love me, my troubled heart remained hidden away in my own secret universe.

In her article, "And the Greatest of These Is Love," Author Sarah Currie, discusses love from a biblical perspective:

> The deepest, most complete, and most demanding type of love, according to the Greeks, was *agape*—selfless, self-giving, empathetic love—extended to all people, whether family members or distant strangers. This is the kind of love which Paul speaks of in 1 Corinthians 13: "If I speak of human eloquence and angelic ecstasy, I'm nothing but the creaking of a rusty gate. No matter what I say, what I believe, and what I do, I'm bankrupt without love. Love never gives up. Love cares more for others than self. Love doesn't want what it doesn't have. Love doesn't strut, doesn't have a swelled head, doesn't force itself on others, doesn't fly off the handle, doesn't keep score of the sins of others; it takes pleasure in the flowering of truth, puts up with anything, always looks for the best, never looks back, but keeps going to the end. Love never dies…(*The Message*, Eugene Peterson).[84]

She elaborates further on love's biblical meaning,

> I know how far from perfect I am, and how inferior to God's way has been my way of loving, so far—and I'm pretty sure that's true of us mere humans. Nevertheless, God has planted within us a longing to love and to be loved, in ways great and small, personal and communal, and I believe

God expects us to keep growing in our capacity to experience and to share love—in all its varieties, but especially in the capacity for *agape*, the greatest of these. Holy Scripture and the teachings of Jesus and all who came after him call us to strive for that ideal, even if on this side of the mortal journey we will inevitably fall short of perfection. *Agape*, unconditional, self-giving, empathetic love, is what we all most need…It's good to remember the heart of our calling: to love one another, as we are so dearly loved by the One who created us, who accompanies us, and who inspires us on our way.[85]

In the opening paragraphs of "Top 6 Definitions of Love That Everyone Should Know," Lisa Smith, a contributor to numerous, online websites, brilliantly encapsulates the significance of the word *love*:

> People say love is pure, painful, sweet, and dreadful—all at once. The truth is that love is a basic necessity in everyone's life. Everyone needs to be loved to live a proper and healthy life. Love has various definitions. Ask someone and they will give you their own definition of love. Love is a variety of feelings, emotions, and attitude. For some, love is more than just being interested physically in someone; it's an emotional attachment.[86]
>
> Love is more of a feeling that a person has for another person. People often confuse love and lust. Love means to be deeply committed and connected to someone. The basic meaning of love is to feel more than just liking someone. It is a bond that two people must share.[87]

* * * * *

Love makes the world go round. Have you ever noticed that the dominant theme of more than half of the lyrics in popular songs is *love*? Lyrics about love may include the most intense feelings of a person's soul or the deepest sadness in a person's heart. Lyrics from a love song can instill a feeling of beautiful romance, or contrarily, intensify the suffering of a broken heart.

Hundreds and hundreds of love songs have been released as popular hit recordings during the timelines of my life. Listening to the lyrics of some is exhilarating and can cause much happiness while listening to the lyrics of others is melancholic and can provoke much sadness.

According to Daniel K. L. Chua, professor of music at the University of Hong Kong, there's no such thing as bad music, and even though music is never played perfectly, there is still a great joy there, however painful it may be. In his article, "Music Is Fundamentally Joy,"[88] he explains that music is calling us to understand our role in creation in a new way:

> I think that music is a call toward relationship, toward a new understanding of what it means to be in the world and to be with one another…Music is about helping us come into relation with the world, with one another, and with creation. I don't think music is instrumental in converting people or anything like that, but it is instrumental in expressing relationship and joy of relationship. Even when it's a lament. There's a fundamental joy that speaks of hope and a faithfulness to God's providential care. Music always points to that in some way; it always tells you not to give up.

"I Want to Know What Love Is," an adult contemporary song performed by the rock group, Foreigner, in 1984, is exemplary of a popular song with music and lyrics consisting of a theme that intimately describes a search for love:

> In my life there's been heartache and pain
> I don't know if I can face it again
> Can't stop now, I've traveled so far
> To change this lonely life
>
> I wanna know what love is
> I want you to show me
> I wanna feel what love is
> I know you can show me[89]

I can easily empathize with those lyrics, especially when thinking back to the 1960s and 1970s when I failed with two relationships that seemed very promising. The first was a whirlwind one and the second was a bittersweet, short-lived one.

Louise and I met in June 1967. We were engaged just three months later and married in May 1968. During the first few years of our marriage, we were a very compatible and satisfied couple, especially after we joyfully celebrated the birth of a daughter in April 1969 and of a son in August 1970. After financial difficulties arose, our relationship started to deteriorate. Shortly before our sixth anniversary, Louise, unwilling to agree to reconciliation to resolve our differences, filed for divorce. Determined to preserve our marriage and to keep our young family intact, I contested the divorce. Unfortunately, our marriage was sadly dissolved in September 1974. Most heartbreaking for me was the overnight awareness of becoming a part-time father to a five-year-old daughter and a four-year-old son. The love for my children was deep and when I realized that I no longer would be sharing time with them on a daily basis, the effect was hurtful and heart-rending. The dissolution of the marriage was very distressing and caused much "heartache and pain," as suggested by the words in the opening lyrics to "I Want to Know What Love Is." My marriage to Louise is chronicled in much greater detail in "Happiness Was Just an Illusion," chapter 8 of *At Last I Open My Heart*.[90]

While rebounding from my failed marriage, I met Nina in May 1975 and immediately became infatuated with her. Though our relationship seemed to hold much promise when it peaked during the summer of 1975, it soon took a dramatic turn for the worse, suddenly ending in February 1976. The heartbreak and despair of our breakup cast a long shadow of darkness on the reckless path that I pursued during the two years that followed.

At times, I still find myself reminiscing about the great love that I once shared with Nina. Although our relationship was brief, I believe that she was not only the greatest love that I ever shared during my life, but also the greatest that I ever lost. Two years after our relationship ended, I was inspired to write the lyrics of a song that I titled "The Bits of a Broken Heart." It was arranged as a country ballad and the words emotionally expressed the heartbreak and pain that I experienced from lost love. Though the song was never successfully published, it appropriately served as a means of closure to the unfortunate ending of my relationship. Our ups and downs, as well as my song lyrics, are journaled in "Looking for Love in Too Many Faces" in chapter 9 of *At Last I Open My Heart*.[91]

The wondrous love that I discovered during the months that I shared with Nina reminds me of the beautiful words of a romantic ballad that was very popular in 1977, "After the Lovin',"[92] which soared to the top of the US *Billboard* chart that year. The song's bittersweet words elicit emotions of happiness as well as sadness. I have listened to them many times and I must confess that I have been deeply moved each time:

> It's hard to explain everything that I'm feelin'
> Face to face I just seem to go dry
> But I love you so much that the sound
> Of your voice can get me high
>
> Thanks for taking me
> On a one way trip to the sun
> And thanks for turning me into someone

So I sing you to sleep after the lovin'
I brush back the hair from your eyes
And the love on your face is so real
That it makes me wanna cry

And I know that my song isn't sayin' anything new
Oh, but after the lovin' I'm still in love with you

In spite of the sad outcome of the relationship that we shared, Nina and I cared deeply for one another. Unfortunately, because of the baggage that I carried, I could not overcome the stigma of feeling that I was an evil, immoral man, often believing that I was unworthy of the great love that Nina had to offer. On the other hand, Nina also battled demons of her own and regrettably became involved in drug use to ease her pain. I cherished our relationship and believed that she was the one woman whose special love would endure forever. Though a lifetime of happiness and joy was not destined for us, I believe that Nina cared about me dearly and that the love we shared together was genuine.

To this day, because Nina was so extraordinarily special to me, I am still moved emotionally when I listen to the following words from, "After the Lovin'": "I brush back the hair from your eyes and the love on your face is so real that it makes me wanna cry." I can still see myself celebrating the bliss of believing that I had discovered genuine love as I gazed into Nina's dark brown eyes—during both the first time and the last. She was a beautiful woman. I loved her dearly, and I will never forget our time together on this earth. I describe our final, tender, heartbroken moments in *At Last I Open My Heart*:

I called out her name one more time but there was no response. I leaned forward and gently brushed her frosted hair away from her eyes. Though her face appeared to be slightly weathered, much of her natural beauty had not faded away. I gently set down the bouquet of red roses, which I had been holding since I arrived at her apartment, on the bedspread a few inches away from her hand. Though she was unable to speak during those moments, she managed to tilt her head upward. Her eyelids were now almost fully open, and she seemed to notice the flowers and recognize me as well. Her hand grazed the bouquet of roses and a faint smile crossed her lips. I was relieved that she was showing signs of semiconsciousness and tears gathered in my eyes when she seemed to be pleased with the bouquet of roses. For an instant, we quietly gazed into each other's eyes. Though she was not completely conscious, I softly caressed her hand with my fingertips, then gently kissed her forehead. Tears rolled down my cheeks as our eyes once again affectionately met.

"I love you, Nina," I whispered to her softly. "I will always love you." Those would be the last words that I would ever say to her. Though I tried to contact her that evening and for weeks afterward, we never reconnected. I only hoped that she discovered true happiness at some point during the decades that followed our relationship. In 2016, forty years after we shared those final moments together, I was very saddened to learn that Nina had passed away several years earlier at the relatively young age of fifty-nine.

From time to time, I find myself thinking back to that sunny day in early May when Nina and I met for the first time. A smile comes to my face as I remember her own sensuous smile and the special glow in the smooth, olive complexion of her face. I can still feel the warm and tender touch of her hand as she held it in mine. I cherish those special memories. We had so much love to offer one another during that wonderful summer of 1975, but our lives were destined to follow different paths. Our relationship may have never become a permanent one, but my life became much more meaningful during the short time that we shared our genuine love together. I loved her very much and I will never forget her. I will never forget the beautiful woman with frosted hair and dark brown eyes. I will never forget Nina.[93]

* * * * *

In an in-depth study of the word *love*, Kara Rosania, while attending Bryn Mawr College in Pennsylvania, submitted an outstanding composition titled *The Beauty of Love*.[94] An eighteen-year-old student at the time, her commendable work thoroughly explores the wonders of love in a delightful and informative style. Here are the opening words of her research paper:

> Love is beautiful. It is the mysterious force that binds people to those around them. It has infinitely many forms, and each of the forms never stays the same for long. Love is always evolving and changing intensity. My own experience with love comes in many forms. I love many people, and many things, all in different ways. It can sometimes be ugly, but it is always beautiful…

She continues to discuss the beauty of love:

> Romantic love, as in all love, can certainly have an ugly side. I have never experienced a love that didn't come with its share of heartache. People forget how dependent they are on each other for happiness and aren't always careful

enough with each other's feelings. People who love each other are more capable of hurting each other than anyone else. That power can be ugly, but power itself can be beautiful. The fact that people have enough faith in another person, in the joys of love, that they allow themselves to be vulnerable to such pain, is a beautiful thing…

The purest form of love, unconditional love, is what I find the most beautiful. My parents love me unconditionally. It is so deep and unchanging, something that exists no matter what else happens in the world. My parents know me better and longer than anyone else in the world. I probably know them better than most people too. There is something beautiful about that, about a connection that exists between people and that will last forever…

Loving others is one of the best ways to become a better person. The love you feel arouses your curiosity and makes you interested in learning more about others, and as a result, the world we live in. When you love someone, you do everything you can to care about them and try to make them happy. This often means sacrificing the things that make you the happiest. Learning to be more giving and selfless is an incredibly beautiful thing…

Kara Rosania's extensive research study also establishes an emotional connection with music. I shared similarities earlier with the lyrics of two love songs, "I Want to Know What Love Is" (1984) and "After the Lovin'" (1977). The lyrics in each of these songs evoke bittersweet, past memories of my own life.

Kara continues with her insightful discussion:

I believe my obsession with music stems from my obsession with love. I write music myself, and I've noticed the songs that turn out much better than others are the ones about love. This can mean love of any kind, the love of other people, the love of life, love of nature, love of a hobby or interest. Love implies passion, and passion inspires beautiful music. When people care about things, they choose words and notes more shrewdly, and are able to create sounds that are entirely unique to a particular song.

As I love music, I also believe that the word *love* can apply to objects, places and experiences. This form of love can serve as a substitute for the love of others when one is all alone. Usually, however, I've noticed that my love of objects and abstracts tend to stem from love of people. For example, I love the sound of the ocean, because it reminds me of being at the beach with my cousins. I love thunderstorms because it reminds me of crawling in bed with my parents, feeling absolutely safe despite the howling on the others side of the window. Our connection with people stem into all aspects of our lives, and make us feel loved even when we are not surrounded by those who care about us most.

Kara's treatise about love brilliantly concludes with these absorbing words:

Perhaps you might say that because I'm only eighteen years old, I couldn't possibly know that much about love. However, I think the wonderful thing about love is that it's something everyone can experience. As you get older, you certainly have more opportunities to love others and to be loved. That doesn't mean that the love I feel, or that a five-year-old feels, is no less an accurate portrayal of what love is. It is whatever I feel it is, as well as whatever that five-year-old feels it is. Love, like beauty, is in the eye of the beholder.

I think the reason that love is such a beautiful thing is because it is a lot like beauty itself. It is that unspeakable connection to certain people or things for unexplainable reasons. It is very abstract, can be hard to describe, and is something that everyone defines differently and applies to many different types of things. It heightens our emotions and makes us feel truly alive. People will never lose their fascination with love, because it is inside us all to feel it, to share it, and to let it fill our lives.

Kara Rosania's research paper is beautifully written and offers each of us a fresh perspective on the phrase, "Love makes the world go round," a common expression that many of us have heard at one time or another.

The Free Dictionary is considered as one of the world's most comprehensive online sources of information. It is a dictionary, a thesaurus, and an encyclopedia wrapped up into one. It includes synonyms and definitions as well as a wide range of specialized topics—legal, medical, and foreign language dictionaries to mention a few. *The Free Dictionary* also includes the largest collection of English idioms in the world and lists thousands of entries from several of the most trusted names in publishing.

When discussing the often-used idiom, "Love makes the world go round," *The Free Dictionary* notes that love, affection, and kindness to others are what seem to make life worth living. It also states that "love makes the world go round," not money or power, and that the only way to truly be happy is to surround yourself with friends and family.[95]

Audrey Heller's view on the significance of love is explained in the thoughtful words of her poem, "Love Makes the World Go Round":

Love is what makes the world go round!
without it, we're an empty shell.
When we have love in our life,
it's very easy to tell.

Your whole demeanor changes,
it reflects in all you do.
You've become more tolerable,
Somewhat mellower too.

We all need to be wanted,
Someone to show us they care.
It's a wonderful feeling,
just knowing someone special is there.

It's an important factor in the way we conduct
ourselves,
if we're happy, we have a glow.
On the other hand, if we're not,
believe me, it will show.

All of us need to be accepted,
it doesn't matter our age or who we are,
And if we're lucky to find that special person,
we'll benefit from it, by far![96]

For me, to feel loved and accepted, to know in my heart that someone truly cares about me, elicits an ecstatic sensation of happiness, and experiencing that wonderful feeling of happiness makes my life richer and much more meaningful. Embracing that attitude of positive well-being has been essential in my life regardless of the setbacks and failures that have caused sadness and disappointment throughout the years. Positive well-being is a condition that allows a person to live his or her life with happiness and meaning, to feel good about what's happening, and to enjoy a sense of connection with others. Maintaining that attitude, I no longer struggle as I once did. I realize that love will always surround me in one form or another.

Thinking back to the relationship that I shared with Nina, though it was both exhilarating and heartbreaking, I certainly understand that I am not the only individual who has ever experienced the wide range of emotions that love can evoke. Another song that effectively touches on the impact that love can have on an individual is "No Love at All,"[97] a mainstream, popular American hit in 1971 that was released as a more popular version the following year. The refrain, repeated several times in the lyrics of the hit song, describes the immense power of love:

> A little bit of love is better than no love
> Even the bad love is better than no love
> And even the sad love is better than no love at all
> Got to believe that
> A little bit of love is better than no love
> Even the bad love is better than no love
> And any kind of love is better than no love at all

The words from Kara Rosania's masterful research paper, *The Beauty of Love*, come to mind: "Romantic love, as in all love, can have an ugly side. I have never experienced a love that didn't come with its share of heartache."

In the previous chapter, "A Woman: Not an Object," Audrey Hepburn, who was recognized not only as a highly accomplished actress but also as a great humanitarian, was quoted regarding her feelings about the true beauty of a woman. She has been credited with another enduring quote as well, this one regarding the nature of love: "We all want to be loved, don't we? Everyone looks for a way of finding love. It's a constant search for affection in every walk of life."

The motion picture film, *New Year's Eve*,[98] is a romantic comedy that features an ensemble cast of characters in a series of several interrelated vignettes. Though the movie was not a critically acclaimed one, the words heard in the voiceover during its closing moments speak loud and clear. One of the movie's main characters summarizes the significance of love in these words:

> Sometimes it feels like there are so many things in the world that we can't control, but it's important to remember the things that we can do like forgiveness, second chances, and fresh starts because the one thing that turns the world from a longing place to a beautiful place is love—love and any of its forms. Love gives us hope.

Love will always give us hope. Each of us will experience many forms of love during our time on this earth and whether those forms result in happiness, comfort, hurt, sadness, or joy, that emotion will always remain an integral part of our lives. No matter how unfair it may sometimes seem, love is still a very beautiful thing.

Love will always make the world go round, and God's love will endure forever (Psalm 136:26), but most important of all, is to remember that God will always be the first and only undisputed author of love.

8

The Promise That I Have in You

Consider it pure joy, my brothers and sisters,
whenever you face trials of many kinds,
because you know that the testing of
your faith produces perseverance.

—James 1:2–3

Since 2015, I have been managing a small business a few blocks away from the downtown district of Elyria, Ohio. As I enter the building each morning, I can't miss seeing the framed plaque that is mounted adjacent to a wall calendar directly above a coffee stand in the reception area of the office. Displayed on the plaque is an anonymously written poem entitled "Don't Quit!":

When things go wrong as they sometimes will,
When the road you're trudging seems all uphill,

When the funds are low, and the debts are high,
And you want to smile, but you have to sigh,
When care is pressing you down a bit—
Rest if you must, but don't you quit.

Success is failure turned inside out,
The silver tints of the clouds of doubt,
And you never can tell how close you are,
It may be near when it seems afar.

So stick to the fight when you're hardest hit,
It's when things go wrong that you mustn't quit!

Wouldn't it be great if those encouraging words applied to each one of us during the course of our lives? We can expect to face many trials during our time on this earth, and some will certainly be more difficult than others. We all struggle with failure and setbacks during our lives. Hopefully, many of us have decided never to quit during the toughest of times. I made up my mind long ago that I would not quit during troubling times. I believe that there is always a glimmer of hope, and that light will always be shining somewhere out there in the darkness.

In her commencement speech, J. K. Rowling, successful British author and creator of the *Harry Potter* series, spoke the following words to Harvard University's graduating class of June 14, 2008: "It is impossible to live without failing at something unless you live so cautiously that you might as well not have lived at all, in which case you have failed by default."

Two months prior to J. K. Rowling's inspirational speech, a fifteen-year marriage that I shared with my second wife, Diana, was legally dissolved in a matter of moments as we silently and solemnly stood next to one another on the second floor of the County Common Pleas Court building in Lorain County, Ohio. And just two months afterward, I quietly observed my sixty-fifth birthday, depressed and lonely and deeply concerned about the uncertainty of my future.

Believing that I had singlehandedly destroyed my marriage, I struggled with a sense of hopelessness, especially since I had a solid history of failing over and over again. Though I managed to make a remarkable recovery from a long, harrowing battle with addiction, the raw truth remained that I continued to struggle with godforsaken demons that constantly reminded me of the immoral behavior that I battled for so many years. Feeling helpless and lost, I seriously wondered whether or not I would ever successfully rebound from a life of significant failure.

In "What Is Failure and How Can We Make the Most of It?"[99] Paula Thompson, a Positive Psychology Coach and an instructor of leadership classes at Pepperdine University in Malibu, California, offers a solid definition of failure and why so many of us are so easily overcome by the thought of it:

> What is failure? We all experience it. But only some people know how to learn from it to be more successful in the future. It's natural to try to avoid things that could end in failure. Failure can be embarrassing and painful to experience. But what is failure exactly? Failure is defined as lack of success or the inability to meet an expectation. The problem is that we can read too much into failure. Too often, we tie it to our sense of self-worth, self-esteem, and self-acceptance. The expectation that we fail to meet is often our own, or one that we've created in our own head. Most of us don't set out looking to fail at anything. And we especially don't want to be labeled as a failure. But maybe that is a mistake in itself. Failure can be useful. We can learn from it, even gain new insights, and do better next time.

Not too long after the dissolution of my marriage to Diana in 2008, I decided that perhaps it was still not too late to turn my life around. I considered my past failures simply as stepping stones to a more successful future. After regaining lost faith, I encouraged myself to move forward and do whatever might be necessary to vindicate myself from all the years that I had sadly wasted away. God gave me the opportunity to repent from a secret, sinful lifestyle and to seek recovery from a brazen life of sexual addiction. He led me toward a path of redemption before it was too late. Once those horrible demons were driven from my spiritually dead soul, I no longer detested myself for all of the terrible mistakes that I had committed. I abandoned the world of darkness in which I once thrived.

I told myself that regardless of the obstacles that I might face, I would never again retreat to that dreadful world of darkness. I would embrace faith and hope and positively move forward with my life one day at a time, reminding myself that regardless of what the future might hold, the dreadful darkness would never overcome the glorious light.

* * * * *

One of the most enjoyable film classics ever produced, *The Wizard of Oz,*[100] released for the first time in theaters in 1939, was reintroduced to America in 1956 as a premiere telecast. Ratings were so successful that the movie then reran on television as an annual tradition for years to come. Eighteen years of age when I first viewed *The Wizard of Oz,* I was not only delighted but captivated by my own imagination as well. Critically acclaimed to be among the greatest motion pictures ever produced, to this day, it remains one of my favorite motion pictures. I am not exaggerating when I confess that since I first viewed it in 1962, I have experienced the magic and wonder of *The Wizard of Oz* no less than twenty-five more times. I have enjoyed this classic film just as much the twenty-fifth time as I have the first.

In his 2009 review of *The Wizard of Oz,* Mick LaSalle, a *San Francisco Chronicle* film critic, declared: "The entire Munchkinland sequence, from Dorothy's arrival to her departure on the Yellow Brick Road, has to be one of the greatest in cinema history—a masterpiece of set design, costuming, choreography, music, lyrics, storytelling, and sheer imagination."[101]

More than sixty years have gone by since I first listened to a chorus of munchkins, the lovable, little inhabitants of the imaginary land of Oz, shouting out to Dorothy, the movie's central character, those electrifying words: "Follow the Yellow Brick Road! Follow the

Yellow Brick Road!" Dorothy, along with her faithful dog, Toto, does exactly that. She follows the mysterious Yellow Brick Road that will eventually lead to Emerald City and of course, the Wizard of Oz himself.

During her adventure along the Yellow Brick Road, Dorothy meets the Scarecrow, the Tin Man, and the Cowardly Lion. Along with these characters, Dorothy bonds to establish a mutual goal of visiting the mighty Wizard of Oz. They collectively believe that the Wizard can fulfill their wishes. Only he has the power to make their dreams come true. Dorothy is lost and wishes to return to her home in Kansas. The Scarecrow wants a brain. The Tin Man wishes for a heart. And the Cowardly Lion lacks courage.

It is an absolute delight to watch the choreographic sequences progressively unfold, especially when the foursome happily join arms and repeatedly and joyously sing "We're off to see the Wizard, the wonderful Wizard of Oz, we hear he is a whiz of a wiz if ever a wiz there was."[102] We never stop rooting for them as they faithfully share their camaraderie throughout their exciting adventure and we are deeply disappointed after their first visit as the Wizard outrightly denies their wishes and are commanded to return with the broomstick of the Wicked Witch before their wishes will be granted.

The *Collins English Dictionary* defines the "yellow brick road" as the road to success and happiness, which Dorothy, the Scarecrow, the Tin Man, and the Cowardly Lion eventually achieve. *The Wizard of Oz* concludes with the wizard enthusiastically fulfilling each wish: a way back home to Kansas for Dorothy, a brain for the Scarecrow, a heart for the Tin Man, and courage for the Cowardly Lion. We celebrate with each one for achieving their ultimate dream. For a few moments, our hearts are significantly touched because these four iconic characters have received what they longed for all along.

The yellow brick road is very symbolic to me as I have often pondered about the direction of my own life. Did I ever truly follow a yellow brick road that could lead to success and happiness?

On its website, Living Well Dying Well explores various themes about how to live during our journey through life. Several key thoughts are shared:

> The journey through life is filled with wonder, challenges, broken hearts, highs and lows, celebrations, special moments, and memories that define our experience as a human. It is these events, planned or unexpected, that impact our travels and define our purpose. To follow the right path and to remain true to ourselves, we try to overcome our obstacles and sometimes we gain meaning and learning from the challenges, and at other times we experience joy. How we react to what we are faced with determines what the rest of our journey through life will be like.[103]

Each of us faces trials, setbacks, disappointments, and failures during our lifetime. It is often quite difficult to persevere through those troubling moments. Kathryn Sandford is a career resilience coach whose primary goal, according to her website,[104] is to empower men and women to discover their strength, courage, and resilience while on their journey of change. She states on her website, "I have been in your place. I've survived tragic loss, cancer, being fired, and failing in business. I have learned how to cope with grief, rejection, and failure, and I've come out at the other end stronger and equipped with the tools to take charge of my life. In her online blog, "How to Persevere (and Get Ahead) When the Going Gets Tough,"[105] she adds these motivational points to further consider:

> There are times in life when we feel discouraged or defeated when life delivers blows that knock us to the ground. The feelings of hopelessness and despair may consume your life for many months as you wonder if you'll ever get back to

feeling happy and safe. This is when it's import-ant to learn how to persevere in life.

The good news is that over time, life can get better, and you can get stronger when you perse-vere. You'll likely look back at these "difficult life events" and realize that they were the catalysts for you to change your life.

The only way for us to live our lives to the fullest is to learn how to have perseverance and deal with the challenges that life throws at us. Surviving these curveballs and pushing through adversity, pain, and feelings of hopelessness and despair are part of the journey for us to learn about who we are. There is no other way to learn how to be resilient, courageous, hopeful, and optimistic about life and our future.

Everyone feels discouraged and defeated at some point in his or her life journey. Some of us find ourselves at this place of despair, and we do not know what to do, so we stop growing and thriving in life. We end up living our lives through regret, fear, pain, disillusionment, and sadness. This is not how we are meant to live… When you are feeling discouraged and life seems tough, don't give up!

In looking back to my own past, I can certainly appreciate the relevance of Kathryn Sandford's purposeful words regarding life's journey. I have learned not only to persevere during the toughest of times, but also to fully embrace the virtues of hope, faith, and love, each proving to be essential throughout my life.

* * * * *

Released in America in 1996, "Shout to the Lord"[106] is among the most popular Christian songs ever written. When Australian singer-songwriter, Darlene Zschech, originally wrote and recorded the words to this inspirational song of praise in 1993, she explained in an interview with *Today's Christian Woman* her motivation for writing it: "I wrote it when I was feeling discouraged. I felt I could either scream and pull my hair out or praise God. The line, *Nothing compares to the promise I have in you,* was something I clung to when circumstances seemed bleak. I think that would ring true with anyone going through tough times."[107] Since 1996, congregations of millions of churchgoers have sung "Shout to the Lord" each Sunday throughout the world.

In the autumn of 2002, Diana and I shared an opportunity to volunteer at a charity concert sponsored by World Vision International, an evangelical, humanitarian organization that provides aid to impoverished children of third-world countries. The highlight of the sold-out concert was during its final moments when an ensemble of notable Christian artists, led by Darlene Zschech, together sang "Shout to the Lord." When the audience was invited to join in, the powerful words of the song resonated thunderously throughout the auditorium. For Diana and myself, shouting out those heartwarming words of praise along with more than one hundred other voices was not only a memorable experience as husband and wife but a very moving one as well. I'll never forget the great joy and peace that we shared as we sang together, worshipping and praising the Lord with these magnificent words:

> My Jesus my Saviour
> Lord there is none like you
> All of my days I want to praise
> The wonders of your mighty love
> "My comfort, my shelter
> Tower of refuge and strength
> Let every breath, all that I am
> Never cease to worship you
> Shout to the Lord all the Earth, let us sing
> Power and majesty, praise to the King
> Mountains bow down and seas will roar

At the sound of your name
I sing for joy at the work of your hands
Forever I'll love you, forever I'll stand
Nothing compares to the promise I have in You

LyricsMode.com is a comprehensive, online resource that provides text lyrics for popular music compositions. Boasting one of the largest archives of song lyrics, it shares meanings and interpretations of lyrics as well. In a brief review of "Shout to the Lord," the website explains that the artist is telling us that the Lord God is the one and only. He is without equal and will always remain that way. Every creation must sing praise because God alone is worthy and there is no other like Him. He is a God who deserves the praise of everyone and everything that he has created. So we should all celebrate by shouting to the Lord![108]

In "God Keeps His Promises,"[109] Jen Thorn, a regular contributor to Love God Greatly, a ministry that provides online Bible studies to women around the world, we are provided this explanation:

Think back with me to the time when the people of God were slaves in Egypt. They were oppressed, weak, and helpless but God promised that he would rescue them and give them a land of their own. So he raised up leaders like Moses and in miraculous and surprising ways led their escape from Pharaoh's reign.

He continued to care and provide for the people as they wandered in the desert by giving them food and water, allowing them to win battles, and continually leading them to their promised land. But throughout their adventure, the Israelites were slow to trust in the Lord. They were quick to complain and it didn't take long for them to build a golden idol of worship.

In Joshua 21:43–45, we see God's grace abound toward Israel despite their rebellion, disobedience, and unbelief. God keeps his promises and eventually leads them into the land He promised from the beginning. What does this mean for us, living thousands of years later?

God has made promises to us and He keeps them…There are too many to list, but when you hold your Bible, you are holding God's promises to you. Some of the spiritual promises are continued forgiveness of sins, our sanctification, supplying us with strength and peace during trials, and preserving us until the end. When God made these promises, they were then and forever unbreakable. His character doesn't allow him to break or go back on His word. He will keep the promises he makes.

But there are a couple of things that we need. First we must have faith. We must believe in God. We must trust that what He says is true and what He promises will come to pass. This can be extremely hard when life has not gone the way that you had envisioned it to go. This leads to the second thing we must possess, which is patience. We know that God's ways are not our ways and that his timing often does not line up with our scheduled plans for life, and so we need to learn to wait.

We must have patience when waiting for God to fulfill his promises to us. James tells us that our faith will be tested in order to prove that it is genuine and often that these trials are a testing of our patience. Are you willing to wait on the Lord or are you trying to force things to happen that end up causing you to sin? Are you angry at God for not complying with your wishes and dreams? Are you frustrated with your spiritual growth or lack of it or the circumstances you find yourself in?

Do you know the promises that God makes to you in the scriptures? We must first become familiar with what God's promises actually are. Then we must pray daily for God to fulfill his promises in our lives and we must ask him to give us the patience we need to wait and trust… Believe God's promises, be strong and brave in the land in which he has strategically placed you and trust Him as you face your battles, always remembering that you'll never fight alone!

As a believer, I have become familiar with several of the biblical promises that God has bestowed upon us. As Jen Thorn suggests in "God Keeps His Promises," we must not only continue to be patient and trust in God but also believe that his promises will ultimately be fulfilled. They will all come to pass. During the darkest days of my life, God was always present. He has always been patient. He has never abandoned me. His love has always been abounding and unconditional.

My greatest promise of all is with God. He has blessed my life with a special purpose and a special plan. I am forever grateful for each day that he gives me on this earth.

9

The Most Precious Gift of All

For you formed my inward parts; You wove me
in my mother's womb. I will give thanks to You,
for I am fearfully and wonderfully made; wonderful
are your works, and my soul knows it very well.

—Psalm 139:13–14

I believe that the most precious gift of all is life. I received that beautiful gift when I took my very first breath in Polyclinic Hospital in Cleveland, Ohio, on August 23, 1943. On that overcast Monday evening, my parents welcomed their firstborn child into the world—a son. During those moments, recognizing only black and white shadows as newborns generally do, I began my celebration of life as a baby boy who would grow up to one day become an adult man. Like millions of others throughout history, the gender assigned to me as a newborn child would be either male or female. That distinction is clearly reflected by these words in the first chapter of the Bible: "God created mankind in his own image…and the image was created male and female" (Genesis 1:27). The role assigned to each of us in life (male or female) is a role naturally determined by our original identity at birth. For the eighty years that I have lived on this earth and for the thousands of years prior to my existence, the differences have been irrefutably apparent: boy or girl, man or woman, male or female.

I cherish the wonderful gift of life. Though others may adamantly disagree, I disregard the premise that I am perhaps an evolutionary, embryonic byproduct randomly evolved during an earlier stage of history. I celebrate my gift of life as a God-given one, and I will continue to accept that belief by faith and without question. I will not compromise my belief and always hold dear that I am divinely created by an awesome and omnipotent God—a Creator, who, before the foundation of time, not only predetermined my existence but billions of others as well.

* * * * *

Michael Stokes Paulsen, distinguished university chair and professor of law at the University of St. Thomas in St. Paul, Minnesota, has written a powerful article, "The Radical Wrongness of Roe,"[110] which appeared in *First Things* magazine. In the article, he passionately shares his view concerning one of the most controversial, social issues in today's culture. In the article, which was written several months prior to June 24, 2022, the date that the United States Supreme Court overturned the landmark 1973 *Roe v Wade* decision, he explains that abortion is generally defined as the deliberate termination of a human pregnancy. His article includes the following insightful and thought-provoking paragraphs:

> In *Roe v Wade*, the Supreme Court created a constitutional right of some human beings to kill other human beings. Specifically, the Court held that the Constitution of the United States creates a substantive individual liberty to procure or perform *an abortion of a human life*—that is, to terminate a woman's pregnancy by killing the living human embryo or fetus gestating in her womb. The Court located this right to kill the human fetus, implausibly, in the Fourteenth Amendment's guarantee that persons are not

deprived of "life, liberty, or property, without due process of law."

Professor Paulsen continues with a discussion of the consequences of abortion:

> It is important to be clear-eyed about one fact: Abortion kills a living human being. There is no doubt about that; it is a simple reality of human biology. Abortion kills a living being, and that living being is a *human* living being—an organism with a biological identity, and life, separate from that of his or her mother. The act of abortion ends a distinct, unique human life.
>
> To be sure, the human embryo or fetus in utero is *dependent on* the mother's body for survival and sustenance until about twenty-four weeks into pregnancy. That is a fact of biological reality, too. But the unborn child is not *part of* the mother's body. He or she—the unborn child is not an *it* but an embryonic boy or girl with an identifiable sex—is an independent life, living within, and dependent on, the mother's body. Nor does the fact of bodily dependence alter the facts that the fetus is a separate human life and that abortion ends that separate life. It merely means that the human being killed by abortion is killed at an early stage in its life cycle. (I am the same biological organism I was as an embryo, a fetus, a newborn, an infant, a toddler, a teenager, and a younger man. If you had terminated my life at any of those stages, you would have been killing *me*.)
>
> *Roe v Wade* created a license to kill. And kill we have: Since *Roe* fashioned a constitutional right to abortion in 1973, there have been approx-

imately sixty-two million abortions in America, a death toll that dwarfs the Nazi Holocaust and exceeds the total loss of American lives in all of our wars combined.

In the closing paragraphs of the article, the aftermath of the 1973 Supreme Court *Roe v Wade* ruling is summarized:

> One can get lost in the weeds of *Roe's* legal and policy radicalism and forget the most important point. That point is not that the decision is legally indefensible, outrageous, doctrinally offensive, and a betrayal of the Court of its constitutional duty—though all this is true. And it is not that the decision legislates a truly extreme pro-abortion legal regime—though that is also true. The most important point is that this lawless, extremist decision has truly monstrous moral consequences: the creation of a constitutional right to kill, and the massacre has ensued. Extremism has consequences. The wages of *Roe's* extraordinary infidelity to the Constitution is death on a massive scale.
>
> In *Dobbs v Jackson Women's Health Organization*, the Supreme Court has an opportunity to repudiate *Roe*. The Mississippi law at issue in *Dobbs* poses a square conflict with the abortion regime of *Roe*. There can be no middle ground here—no compromise between right and wrong, no trimming on the basis of politics, no pretext of hiding behind "precedent," no perpetuation of constitutional error in any form to any degree. *Roe v Wade* is one of the worst constitutional decisions of all time, if not the worst—an atrocity almost beyond comprehension. To acquiesce in *Roe* is to acquiesce in an American holocaust.

To deny *Roe's* death toll is to engage in a form of holocaust denial. It is time for *Roe* to be decisively and definitively overturned.

Mother Teresa, the late twentieth-century Catholic nun who dedicated her life to assisting the poor and was awarded the Nobel Peace Prize in 1979 for her work involving the struggle to overcome world poverty and distress, is credited with this quote: "It is a poverty to decide that a child must die so that you may live as you wish."

Despite much criticism and controversy surrounding a majority of Mother Teresa's beliefs, she boldly expressed opinions directly from her heart. In February 1997, at the National Prayer Breakfast in Washington, DC, attended by many dignitaries, including the United States President and the First Lady, the outspoken, humanitarian nun passionately poured out her feelings with these powerful words: "What is taking place in America is a war against the child. And if we accept that the mother can kill her own child, how can we tell other people not to kill one another?"

Another of Mother Teresa's controversial and explosive quotes, which triggered much consideration and attention, was published in the *Wall Street Journal* in 1994:

America needs no words from me to see how your decision in *Roe v Wade* has deformed a great nation. The so-called right to abortion has pitted mothers against their children and women against men. It has sown violence and discord at the heart of the most intimate human relationships. It has aggravated the derogation of the father's role in an increasingly fatherless society. It has portrayed the greatest of gifts—a child—as a competitor, an intrusion, and an inconvenience. It has nominally accorded mothers unfettered dominion over the independent lives of their physically dependent sons and daughters. And in granting this unconscionable power, it has exposed many women to unjust and selfish demands from their husbands or other sexual partners. Human rights are not a privilege conferred by government. They are every human being's entitlement by virtue of his or her humanity. The right to life does not depend, and must not be declared to be contingent on the pleasure of anyone else, not even a parent or a sovereign.[111]

Mother Teresa's courageous stand on human life is very commendable. In my opinion, abortion should not be condoned. I believe that God has placed significant value on all human life that was created in his image. This holds true for unborn life as well. I view the conception of a human being as a God-given right to life. The choice to end an unborn child's life should not be an arbitrary one. Other suitable options may be available that can prevent the systematic termination of a child in its fetal stages. All too often, the motive for the choice to abort an unborn child seems to be a selfish one. As a believer, I will not compromise my views on this controversial and volatile issue. I regard my life and all other human life as a valuable and precious gift from God.

* * * * *

R. L. Adams is a successful, published author of many books that offer much inspiration and encouragement. On his website, he has posted "8 Reasons Why Life Is So Precious." He begins by telling us that life is so precious that rather than allowing the sands of time to slip through our hands, we should instead seize the moment:

> We have difficulties with enjoying what we have in the present. We often find ourselves longing for something else, never really savoring what we have right now, in this very moment. And, often, it takes some calamity or major strife for us to realize the fragility of life, and just how pre-

cious we all are in the yes of someone near and dear to our hearts.

It shouldn't take massive amounts of pain to open our eyes to the beauty of what we have. We tend to allow the miracles that are happening all around us to fall by the wayside as we sit and wallow, immersed in fear, replete with stress and anxiety. No, it shouldn't work like that. But we all know that it does. We all take this precious life for granted at one point or another in our lives. Yes, all of us.

However, if you've landed here, then there's a reason why you're reading these words. I believe that everything in life happens for a reason. No matter what it is, there is a divine purpose. We might not always realize it at the moment, especially when we're dealing with massive amounts of pain or failure, but there is.

And the simple fact will always remain that no matter what happens—no matter what trials or tribulations you have to dredge through—that life will always be precious. We just have to find the good in every moment, no matter how meek or meager it might seem to us, because everything in life is subjective, gleaned upon by the status quo in our lives. The problem with that, we don't look to what we have. Rather, we're deluged with a flood of thoughts immersed in what we don't have. We envy others for enjoying success and the fruits of their labors while we live in a tormented state of pity, regret, and anger. It bothers us when people around us succeed. It bothers us that our seemingly small problems seem so big.

Today, right now, at this very moment, there are people enduring a tremendous amount of strife. When you stop to think about it for a moment, there is an enormous amount of pain and suffering happening everywhere. The sheer enormity of it all can certainly feel overwhelming. However, the plight of others should remind us about the importance of the simple beauties and treasures in our own lives. Instead of looking to the haves, we must look to the have-nots as a reminder of what we do have and what we don't have. We have to get off the Hedonic Treadmill and become more attuned to the preciousness in every moment of time.

The fact of the matter remains that we're here one moment and gone the next. If we spend that infinitesimal amount of time steeped in worry and negative emotions, we'll never realize the miraculous gift of life that we've been given. If you think about the probability of life and our own existence, you'll realize why every moment needs to be savored and treated like it could be our last. However, all of this is just talk. To the person who is suffering through the torment of failure or has entirely lost hope in life, these are just words. The words might invoke some emotions, but they're ultimately overpowered by the burden of thousands of pounds of problems resting like the weight of the world on our shoulders.

Yet, no matter what the present situation might be in your life—no matter how many problems might exist—this too shall pass. And in that time, your faith must remain unwavering.[112]

R. L. Adams offers several additional reasons that remind us about the preciousness of our lives:

The thing about life is that whatever we tend to focus on, we move toward. When we think that life is a curse or merely a painful struggle, we manifest that more into our lives. We find more experiences that help to prove our theory over time. With every additional experience, and every added ounce of focus toward the end, we continue its manifestation in our lives. When you realize that life is precious, you also look at everything with childlike pleasure, as though you were experiencing it for the first time. It shouldn't take a near death experience or some other major calamity in life to realize how important human life is no matter what our present situations, skin color, religion, gender, or what anything else is for that matter.

Oftentimes, when we fail, we have difficulty realizing just how precious life might be. We focus on the failures and it consumes us, eating away at us mentally, emotionally, spiritually, and physically. But life's failures aren't designed to do that. They're designed to allow us to grow and learn invaluable lessons that can only be gleaned through those very failures. Failure at anything, no matter how big or small it might be, should help to open our eyes to the absolute importance of what we've been given—a chance to live, breathe, and experience life in the physical realm. Never take that for granted no matter how bad your failures might be nor how small they may make you feel. There's a reason for it all.[113]

Even in situations of great pain and anguish, we should realize the fragility of life, its importance, and its meaning. While pain can dampen the body, it enriches the mind over time. Through pain we grow and learn. We become more aware of our surroundings and gain a deeper understanding of the purpose of our lives. No matter what occurs, nor how much pain it inflicts, it should help enhance our awareness of whatever it is that we want or desire. Pain can dramatically change the course of our lives, but oftentimes, it's a refinement of direction. Don't allow pain to destroy you; rather, allow it to uplift you and make you realize how important life really is.[114]

When things don't quite go according to our plans, we lose hope. When everything around us is shattered into a million pieces, it's hard to keep an elevated spirit. But, rather than fill our minds with negativity, we need to be grateful for what we do have, no matter what it is. Because, through gratitude, we appreciate the beauty of the lives we've been blessed with. Gratitude is also the pathway to hope. When we're grateful, we move out of a state of fear, and move into a state of love and compassion. We can be more sympathetic and empathetic, and those positive energies rejuvenate and replenish the spirit rather than taking it away.[115]

We often fail to appreciate just how precious life is when we compare ourselves to others. Whether we compare financially or through some other aspect, we look to what we don't have rather than what we do have. There will always be people to compare to and who are more successful or powerful or attractive or whatever else you might have. But you can't compare yourself to them. Your life is unique. You're on a unique journey meant to take unique discoveries in life. Your time shouldn't be spent dwelling on what you don't have. Appreciate the journey. Take a walk and smell the roses. That's what matters. But don't compare yourself to others if you want to have any semblance of happiness or peace whatsoever. Happily succeed rather than trying to succeed to be happy.[116]

The author also shares his own remarkable story about the motivation that led to his success:

> I started my website in the middle of 2014, but it has now grown beyond anything that I had envisioned, reaching an audience of millions of people around the world. And so many of you write to me asking me questions every single day without fail. Often, I find myself responding back with similar responses. But to sum things up, in 2011, my life fell apart…I guess you could say that I failed in a major way. My business came crashing down. My marriage ended, and everyone who I had once considered a so-called friend, bailed out on me. Decimated doesn't even describe the state and quality of my life at the time. I was left with nothing. It was the lowest point of my existence…And I knew things had to change.
>
> I wanted to improve my life. I wanted things to get better. But I had no idea how I was going to move forward from the lowest point in my life and pick up the broken pieces. All I really knew was that I wanted more in life than the incessant rollercoaster ride of failure and success…I was done with that.
>
> Even though I was nearly homeless at the time with very little hope left in the world, somehow I mustered the courage to move forward and learn. But the process was brutal. I wandered around aimlessly for a couple of years, not really knowing what I wanted to do with my life. It was around that point that I locked myself up in

a room and started to write. I'm not sure where it all came from, but it just flowed out of me. Over the course of the next eighteen months, I managed to write three dozen books. I built up a massive, passive income stream and created numerous courses and niche websites. Afterward, I started traveling the world, spending nearly two years in foreign countries. That's where I met my beautiful wife and had two precious children who are my world.

To say that I have learned a lot is an understatement. I dove deep into who I really was as a person. I cut everything else out of my life. Not a single toxin entered my body since then. Not one. The amount of laser-guided focus that I was able to instill in myself is nothing short of a miracle. I have no idea where it came from, but I had this burning desire to share what I learned with others.[117]

R. L. Adams story is an inspirational and triumphant one and much can be learned from it regarding the meaningfulness and preciousness of our lives.

* * * * *

Most of us recognize this phrase, "Life, liberty, and the pursuit of happiness." It appears in the United States Declaration of Independence of 1776. This historical document reminds us that "life, liberty, and the pursuit of happiness" are unalienable rights given to all humans by their Creator. Not many of us would deny the pursuit of happiness in our lives. Happiness is that feeling that comes over you when you know life is good, and you can't help but smile. It's the opposite of sadness and creates a sense of well-being, joy, or contentment. When people are successful, safe, or lucky, they feel happiness. Whenever doing something that causes happiness, people usually want to do more of it. No one ever complained about experiencing too much happiness.[118]

Pete Wiley, author of *Blocks of Life*, regularly shares his thoughts with a wide audience through his website, blocksoflife.com. He provides us with some interesting insights in his blog, "The Foundation of Happiness—Bringing Happiness to Others by Making Yourself Happy First."

It feels good when people like you and admire you. The need for this stems from a fundamental and deep-seated desire to be loved. One way to make people love you is to contribute to their happiness. No one can make someone else happy if they don't want to be happy, but it is possible to create conditions that give people a better chance at happiness. For example, think of the people you look forward to being with. What is it about them that makes you want to be with them? Chances are that something in your interaction with them enhances your self-image or confidence. They may challenge you intellectually and make you think. They may take an interest in your life and how you are doing. They may be funny. They may be accepting of who you are—people you can be yourself with. Any of these things have the potential to make you happier.

If we try to make others happy because it gives us something back—it makes us feel good about ourselves or gives our lives meaning—that's very good. Perhaps we only do it because if we make other people happy, they will like us, and only if they like us will we be convinced that we are likable, then this is not good. We have to be comfortable with who we are *first*. Instead of making people happy in order to get external validation of our worthiness, we should be worthwhile for *us*. Only by building on this foundation can we contribute toward other people's happiness in a sincere way.

You have to strive to be the best version of yourself for your own sake—to make *you* happy… There's nothing inherently wrong with doing something to make other people like you, but you should spend most of your time doing things for you. Making choices for you helps you develop the best version of yourself. If you are the best version of yourself for your sake, you can be the best version of yourself when interacting with others. Your interactions will be more genuine, and, ultimately, you'll have a greater positive impact on the world around you.[119]

* * * * *

During the early 2000s, while I attended Church of the Open Door in Elyria, Ohio, I participated in a drama ministry known as the Boiling Point Players. Performing with the ensemble group turned into a great passion of mine. A friend suggested that I join the ministry in 2002, not long after I began my recovery from decades of harrowing addiction. Serving and performing in the drama ministry for nearly seven years was very special during a crucial time of my life.

For many years, I have been blessed to support Cornerstone, a pro-life ministry founded in Elyria, Ohio in 1986, that provides life-affirming services for women. In the autumn of 2008, I was approached by Cornerstone's board president and asked if I would be willing to consider the possibility of organizing and creating a fundraising event that would benefit Cornerstone Among Women, which was the ministry's name during its earlier years. Though efforts to successfully create the event were originally thwarted, another opportunity would arise several months later that I would cherish as a special blessing during that time in my life.

As a former member of the Boiling Point Players, I performed in several events that were presented by the drama ministry at Church of the Open Door. My first performance was staged in a large-scale event titled "A Sundae with Nuts" during the summer of 2003. A few hundred people attended the production that featured performances in a dozen different skits. One of the audience's favorites was "Can I Get a Witness," which consisted of a series of humorous vignettes demonstrating how a Christian should not witness to an unbeliever. The interchanges in each of the sketches between the characters portrayed by a few other cast members and myself were very effective and entertaining as well. I also wrote the script and starred in a lead role of another sketch that was staged that evening. "Do You Hear What I Hear?" featured a pair of unforgettable, lovable, bumbling Christian senior men exchanging hilarious quips while drinking coffee at a food court in the middle of a crowded shopping mall. The audience was delighted by the feel-good performances. "A Sundae with Nuts" was a huge success that evening.

One of my more memorable roles as a Boiling Point Player was in a murder mystery production, "You Have the Right to Remain Dead," which was presented in October 2004. The character I portrayed was the flamboyant Fat Daddy, confined to a wheelchair complete with a straw hat and endowed with an unforgettable southern drawl. The audience was well entertained by the murder mystery presentation, affirming their appreciation that evening by delivering a standing ovation to our entire ensemble of players.

Entertaining an audience and knowing that I could bring joy, laughter, and happiness into the lives of others added a special sense of accomplishment during my participation in the drama ministry. To this day, I still hold dear a heartwarming letter in which I was commended by the talented director of sketches that included my performances of many different characters. She presented me with this endearing message:

"Dear Bart: Hi! I just wanted to let you know what a valued member you are to the Boiling Point Players. Your willingness to serve, your creativity in writing and many other areas, and your determination to define your characters are all assets that you bring to the body of our drama ministry. Keep up the good work, "Fat Daddy," and I know that your impossible prayers will be lifted up.

I appreciated Nancy's encouragement very much. Sadly, she passed away only a few years after she wrote that emboldening message. I credit her with much of my success in the drama ministry. Her recognition of my acting potential motivated me significantly, especially during the early months of 2008 when I was first asked about the possibility of creating a fundraiser for the Cornerstone ministry. Though the initial effort had failed months earlier, I became more determined than ever to revisit the possibility of spearheading a successful fundraiser. I telephoned the chief executive officer of Cornerstone Among Women at the time, and we agreed to meet in a couple of weeks to resurrect our discussion to hold a fundraiser event.

I conferred with Rich Hales, who had also served as a longtime member of the Boiling Point Players ministry at Church of the Open Door. Our drama group had unfortunately disbanded a few years earlier after the unexpected termination of the ministry. Rich, too, had a genuine passion for performing in many of our drama events and he equally expressed interest in resuming efforts to develop a fundraiser. Our first meeting with Cornerstone Among Women was in early February of 2009.

After months of collaboration and planning, the fundraising event was a *go*. We scheduled it for September 20, 2009, recreating it as a revival of "A Sundae with Nuts," which had originally been staged by the Boiling Point Players six years earlier. Performances would now be by members of our newly formed group, the New Life Players. Our pro-life theme would consist of sixteen sketches. The first was titled "No More Womb" and was about two preborn children in their embryonic stages conversing with one another while sharing concerns of their imminent birth and future life on earth. The last sketch was titled "Love, Octogenarian Style" and was about an eighty-one-year-old Italian father, a widower overcome with joy and happiness about marrying for a second time. That closing sketch, with delightful dialogue between Rich Hales as the subtle, troubled son, and myself, as the broken-accented, spunky, Italian father, was among the evening's favorites.

Also included in the presentation was a sketch entitled "Love Is a Cliché," which was applauded by the audience with cheers and laughter. The sketch illustrated how a combination of romantic love and music can create a somewhat twisted message about the true meaning of love. The skit portrays a husband and wife whose fifteen-year marriage is unsettled and fading away and consists of lines that are lyrics from popular hit songs of the 1960s, 1970s, and 1980s, which I volunteered to select to appropriately fit in the dialogue between the husband and wife. I was cast as the rambunctious husband in one of my favorite performances of the evening. The reception of the skit by the audience was an absolute delight.

The fundraiser was enjoyed by all those who attended and turned into a great success. In her letter of appreciation delivered shortly afterward, the chief executive officer of Cornerstone Among Women, wrote:

Dear Bart, Rich, and all New Life Players,

It is hard to describe the feelings of pure joy, admiration, respect, and thankfulness we, from Cornerstone, experienced during the performance of "A Sundae with Nuts." We were wonderfully surprised by the amazing caliber of every aspect of the performance. The passion that kept the dream alive all these months was so evident in the professional, intentional, and artistic execution of the event. May we please extend our heartfelt gratitude to each one involved in this labor of love?

Special thanks to you, Bart, and you, Rich, for spearheading the effort. It was a delight to have our regular update meetings, even though behind the scenes we know you were all counting the cost of creating, producing, and executing this story of life in every season.

So many deserve our thanks for the countless hours of practice and organization. The event could not have been better, except that we wish even hundreds more could have attended this inspiring and entertaining afternoon.

We continue to recount the wonderful moments from following the young couple from birth through life, and all the other relevant vignettes so artfully portrayed. The song medley was masterful! There were so many other moments that made "A Sundae with Nuts" a Sunday to remember.

Though the generous amount raised for the effort expended may not be large in our human eyes, I say again, our Audience of One will no doubt give you the best Review on earth for what you offered to Him for the least of these.

With sincere thanks, Linda

Two days earlier, Linda emailed me to personally express her thanks and admiration for my effort in helping to make the fund-raising event possible:

Hi, Bart. I left a message on your phone but can't wait to see you in person and give you thanks for the heroic effort you especially put forth on our behalf.

I am shocked and thrilled at your suggestion of making this an annual event. That means so much after what you all went through to make this so wonderful and professional in every way. I never imagined so much talent could be concentrated in this group of awesome people.

And you, sir, were in your element. It was a joy to observe! If I were an "announcer," I would announce "Bart Mercurio, the Master of the Masterpiece, the Maestro of the Magnificent!' God bless you back in so many ways for this wonderful gift to the center!

As I think back, the opportunity for me to partner with Cornerstone Among Women to stage such a beautiful pro-life event would never have happened had I not received that precious miracle of life in the first place. I am grateful that throughout my life, friends like Linda, and hundreds of others as well, have divinely crossed my path. Whether performing as an actor or having an opportunity to inspire others through word or song, knowing that I am making the lives of others brighter results in untold joy.

I will always cherish the magnificent miracle of life, and I thank God for endowing me with the special gifts that have enabled me to reach out to those who are struggling or feeling lost, unwanted, or unloved.

Though I squandered away a substantial part of my life, God never abandoned me. Though I once believed that my life was a total failure, God never gave up on me. He has always been there to comfort me and to unconditionally protect me. He created me in his own image with a special purpose and plan in mind.

Not long ago, I came across these anonymous words:

> Whenever you find yourself doubting how far
> you can go,
> just remember how far you have come.
> Remember everything you have faced,
> all the battles you have won,
> and all the fears you have overcome.

Those defining words are a reminder of God's wonderful gifts. During my lifelong journey, whenever I experienced hopelessness or despair, God has been there to comfort me. Though both of my marriages failed, I have celebrated the joy of raising two beautiful children whom I will always love dearly. Though I have endured the desolation of years of financial hardship, I have rebounded and have been blessed with my own successful business.

Well into the autumn of my life, I am grateful that God has provided me with the tools needed to share my testimony with others so that they too may discover hope during their darkest of hours. I am a blessed man, and I cherish God's most precious gift of all—the miracle of life.

I will continue to embrace faith and hope because I know and believe that the light will always shine in the dark.

Endnotes

Chapter 1: Faith Over Fear

1 Rindlisbacher, Samuel, "Peace in a Restless Time," *Midnight Call,* July 2020: 6–13.

2 Mercurio, Bart V., *At Last I Open My Heart* (Meadville, Pennsylvania: Christian Faith Publishing, Inc., 2019).

3 Schilling, Terry, "How Big Porn is Making the Coronavirus Crisis Even Worse," thefederalist.com/2020/04/03/how-big-porn-is-making-the-coronavirus-even-worse/>, April 3,2020.

4 Ibid.

5 Ibid.

6 Ibid.

Chapter 2: That Was Then, This Is Now

7 Mercurio, Bart V., *At Last I Open My Heart,* Chapter 11, "I Know I'll Never Find Another You," 165, (Meadville, Pennsylvania: Christian Faith Publishing, Inc., 2019).

8 Mercurio, Bart V., *At Last I Open My Heart,* Chapter 12, "Once I Was Lost…Now I Am Found," 191–2, (Meadville, Pennsylvania: Christian Faith Publishing, Inc., 2019).

9 Ibid, 192.

10 Ibid, 192.

11 Ibid, 192.

Chapter 3: Evil That Was Meant for Good

12 Mercurio, Bart V., *At Last I Open My Heart,* Chapter 13, "At Last I Open My Heart," 200 (Meadville, Pennsylvania: Christian Faith Publishing, Inc., 2019).

Chapter 4: A Perfect Storm

[13] "Coronavirus & Lockdown on Porn Industry," www.inventiva.co.in/trends/coronavirus-lockdown-impact-on-porn-industry/>, April 25, 2020.

[14] Baumgardner, Julie, "What You Need to Know about the Pandemic and Porn," First Things First, blog, https://firstthings.org/what-you-need-to-know-about-the-pandemic-and-porn/, August 12, 2020.

[15] Ibid.

[16] Ibid, "Coronavirus and Porn."

[17] Ibid, "The Impact of Porn Addiction."

[18] Ibid.

[19] Ibid.

[20] Batcho, Kristi I., PhD, "Too Much Pleasure, Not Enough Happiness," *Psychology Today*, blog, https://psychologytoday.com/us/blog/longing-nostalgia/201903/too-much-pleasure-not-enough-happiness/, March 19, 2019.

[21] Ibid.

[22] Ibid.

[23] Bennett, Carole, MA, *Reclaim Your Life—You and the Alcoholic/Addict*, Chapter 1, "The Most Common Routes Leading to Addiction," (Santa Barbara, California: Sea Hill Press, Inc., 2010).

[24] Ibid, Chapter 1.

[25] Ibid, Chapter 1.

[26] "Perfect storm," Origin (Wikipedia, the free encyclopedia), https://en.wikipedia.org/wiki/Perfect_Storm

[27] Akers, Shawn A., "The Destructive Force That Enslaves a Large Portion of the Church," htpps://charismanewscom/marketplace/75763-the-destrucive-force-that-enslaves-a-large-portion-of-the-church, March 29, 2019.

[28] Gibbons, Luke/Kingdom Works, "15 Statistics About the Church and Pornography That Will Blow Your Mind," https://www.charismanews.com/us/73208–15-statistics-about-the-church-and-pornography-that-will-blow-your-mind, September 18, 2018.

[29] Ibid.

[30] Ibid.

Chapter 5: For Such a Time as This

[31] Evans, Dr. Tony, "For Such a Time as This," https://proverbs31.org/read/devotions/full-post/2019/01/14/for-such-a-time-as-this, January 14, 2019.

[32] Ibid.

[33] Ibid.

[34] *Enduring Word Bible Commentary*, https://enduringword.com/bible-commentary/esther-4/, (Enduring Word Ministries, David Guzik, Goleta, California), 2018

[35] Hildreth, D. Scott, *Bondage and Freedom: Escaping the Trap of Pornography*, (Nashville, Tennessee: Holman Bible Publishers, 2018).

[36] Hildreth, D. Scott, "4 Effective Ways to Escape the Grip of Pornography," https://outreachmagazine.com/features/discipleship/55243–4-ways-to-escape-the-grip-of-pornography.html, May 7, 2020.

[37] Ibid. ("Will You Walk in Faith or Try to Do It Your Own Way?"

[38] Ibid. ("1. Realize the Destructiveness of Pornography").

[39] "Steps to Overcome Porn Addiction," pathwaysreallife.com/steps-overcome-pornography-addiction/ (Pathways Real Life Recovery, Sandy, Utah).

[40] Ibid. ("Steps to Overcome Porn Addiction"), Introduction.

[41] Ibid. ("Steps to Overcome Porn Addiction,") "Understanding Healthy Sexuality."

[42] Ibid. ("Steps to Overcome Porn Addiction"), "Recognizing the Signs of Pornography Addiction"; "Treating the Underlying Causes."

[43] Cline, Victor B. (1925–2013), "The Pornography Trap," *Marriage and Families*, Vol. 9, Article 3. Available at: https://scholarsarchive.byu.ed/marriageandfamilies/vol9/iss1/3(2002).

[44] Ibid. "The Pornography Trap": Escalation."

[45] Mercurio, Bart V., *At Last I Open My Heart* (Meadville, Pennsylvania, Christian Faith Publishing, Inc., 2019), Chapter 6: "Amazing Grace…How Sweet the Sound," 75–76.

[46] Mercurio, Bart V., *At Last I Open My Heart* (Meadville, Pennsylvania, Christian Faith Publishing, Inc., 2019), Chapter 8: "Happiness is Just an Illusion," 102.

[47] Mercurio, Bart V., *At Last I Open My Heart* (Meadville, Pennsylvania, Christian Faith Publishing, Inc., 2019), Chapter 9: "Looking for Love in Too Many Faces," 126–127.

[48] Blangiardo, Tom, "The Poison of Pornography," Pure Life Ministries, May 21, 2019, https://purelifeministries.org/blog/the-poison-of-pornography

[49] "Effects of Pornography," Marripedia—https://www.maripedia.org/effects_of_pornography. Last Update: May 30, 2017.

[50] Report of the APA Task Force on the Sexualization of Girls, American Psychological Association, Washington, DC, 2008, at http://www.apa.org/pi/wpo/sexualizationrep.pdf; and: National Campaign to Prevent Teen and Unplanned Pregnancy: "SEX and TECH, Washington, DC, 2008, at http:www.thenationalcampaign.org/SEXTECH/PDF/SexTech_Summary.pdf.

[51] Gibbons, Luke, "How Pornography is Linked to Human Trafficking," *Charisma News*, https:apprequest.charismanews.com/opinion/74424-how-pornogaphy-is-linked-to-human-trafficking, December 13, 2018.

[52] Ibid.

[53] Ibid., "So How is Pornography Connected."

[54] Ibid.

[55] Ibid., "But I'm Just Watching a Few Porn Videos on My Computer."

[56] Ibid.

57 Tennis, Taylor, "Porn and Human Trafficking: The Facts You Need to Know," August 26, 2021; https:/theexodusroad.com/porn-and-human-trafficking-the-facts-you-need-to-know/

58 Ibid., "How are Porn and Human Trafficking Related?"

59 Ibid.

60 Ibid., "What Trafficking Looks Like in the Porn Industry."

61 Ibid., "What About Porn Content on Free Websites?"

62 Fight the New Drug (FTND), "9 Surprising Facts About Human Trafficking in the U.S.," December 14, 2021), https://fightthenewdrug.org/surprising-facts-about-human-trafficking-in-the-u-s/

63 *Sound of Freedom*, Dir. Alejandro Monteverde; Perf. Jim Caviezel, Mia Sorvino (Angel Studios, 2023).

64 Yenor, Scott, "Sexual Counter-Revolution," *First Things*, November 2021.

65 (Hepburn, Audrey 1929—1993), https://en.wikipedia.org/wiki/Audrey_Hepburn

66 Levenson, Sam 1911—1980), *In One Ear and Out the Other*, (Boston, MA: G.K. Hall & Co, 1974).

67 Ray, Sanjana, "Why Audrey Hepburn Will Always Be More Than Just a 'Pretty Face'," https:yourstory.com/2017/05/life-of-audrey-hepurn/amp, May 4, 2017

68 Ibid.

Chapter 6: A Woman: Not an Object

69 Thomas, Geoffrey, "And God Created Woman," June 15, 2006; https://banneroftruth.org/us/resources/articles/2006/and-God-created-woman/

70 Ibid. founded in 2009), Salt Lake City, Utah, https:fightthenewdrug.org/hugh-hefner-dead-at-91/

71 Mercurio, Bart V., *At Last I Open My Heart* (Meadville, Pennsylvania, Christian Faith Publishing, Inc.,2019), Chapter 5: "Once I Had a Secret Love," 60.

72 Mercurio, Bart V., *At Last I Open My Heart*, Chapter 2, "A Gifted Child…a Troubled Man," 34, (Meadville, Pennsylvania: Christian Faith Publishing Inc., 2019).

73 The Lettermen, "The Way You Look Tonight," Capitol Records, 1961, (lyrics by Dorothy Fields, Music by Jerome Kern).

74 Mercurio, Bart V., *At Last I Open My Heart* (Meadville, Pennsylvania: Christian Faith Publishing, Inc., 2019).

75 *Notting Hill*, Dir. Roger Mitchell, Perf. Julia Roberts, Hugh Grant. Universal Pictures, 1999.

76 *Fireproof*, Dir. Alex Kendrick, Perf. Kirk Cameron, Erin Bethea. Samuel Goldwyn Films, Affirm Films, 2008.

77 *City for Conquest*, Dir. Anatole Livak, Perf. James Cagney, Ann Sheridan. Warner Brothers, 1940, https://en.wikipedia.org/wiki/City-for-Conquest.

Chapter 7: Love Makes the World Go Round

78 Lehmiller, Justin, PhD, *Tell Me What You Want: The Science of Sexual Desire and How It Can Help You Improve Your Sex Life*, (New York, NY 10104, Hachette Book Group Inc., 2020), https//:www.healthline.com/health/relationships/difference-between-love-and-lust#common-definitions.

79 Mercurio, Bart V., *At Last I Open My Heart*, Chapter 10, "How Can a Worthless Man Ever Be Loved?" 141–2, (Meadville, PA: Christian Faith Publishing, Inc., 2019).

80 Ibid, 141–2.

81 Ibid, 141–2.

82 Ibid, 141–2.

83 Ibid, 142.

84 Currie, Sarah, "And the Greatest of These is Love. 1 Corinthians 13:13," (Eden Hill Communities), https://edenhill.org/and-the-greatest-of-these-is-love-1-corinthians-13/31, January 25, 2019.

85 Ibid.

86 Smith, Lisa, "Top 6 Definitions of Love That Everyone Should Know," (Paragraph 1), https://www.lifehack.org/310399/top-6-definitions-of-love-that-everyone-should-know.

87 Ibid, (Paragraph 2).

88 Chua, Daniel K.L., "Music Is Fundamentally Joy, Says This Professor of Music"; *US Catholic*, Volume 86, No. 4, April 2021: 16–19.

89 Foreigner, "I Want to Know What Love Is," *Agent Provocateur*, lyrics by Mick Jones, Atlantic Records, 1984, https://en.wikipedia.org/wiki/I_Want_to_Know_What_Love_Is.

90 Mercurio, Bart V., *At Last I Open My Heart*, Chapter 8, "Happiness Was Just an Illusion," 100–110, (Meadville, Pennsylvania: Christian Faith Publishing Inc., 2019).

91 Ibid., Chapter 9, "Looking for Love in Too Many Faces," 115–125 (Nina), 130–132, (Lyrics to "The Bits of a Broken Heart").

92 Humperdinck, Engelbert, "After the Lovin'," *After the Lovin'*, Epic Records, 1977, (lyrics by Alan Bernstein, music by Ritchie Adams), https://en.wikipedia.org/wiki/After_the_Lovin'%27.

93 Mercurio, Bart V., *At Last I Open My Heart*, Chapter 9, "Looking for Love in Too Many Faces," 124–125, (Meadville, PA: Christian Faith Publishing Inc., 2019).

94 Rosania, Kara, "The Beauty of Love," by Serendip, May 2, 2018. https://serendipstudio.org/sci_cult/courses/beauty/web1/krosania.html

95 *The Free Dictionary* (by Farlex, Inc.), https://idioms.thefreedictionary.com/love+makes+the+world+go+round.

96 Heller, Audrey, "Love Makes the World Go Round," July 6, 2008. https://ozofe.com/audrey-heller/love-makes-the-world-go-round.

97 Thomas, B. J., "No Love at All," *No Love at All*, Scepter, 1971, cover version. Lyrics and music by Johnny Christopher and Wayne C. Thompson, 1970). First recorded by Lynn Anderson, *No Love at All*, Columbia, 1970), https://en.wikipedia.org/wiki/No-Love-at-All.

98 *New Year's Eve*, Dir. Gary Marshall. Perf. Sarah Jessica Parker, Jessica Biel. Warner Bros. Pictures, 2011.

Chapter 8: The Promise That I Have in You

99 Thompson, Paula, EdD, "What is Failure and How Can We Make the Most of It?" https://www.betterup.com/blog/what-is-failure, August 18, 2021

100 *The Wizard of Oz*, Dir. Victor Fleming, Perf. Judy Garland, Frank Morgan, Ray Bolger, Bert Lahr, Jack Haley. Metro-Goldwyn-Mayer, 1939.

101 *The Wizard of Oz (1939* film), https://en.wikipedia.org/wiki/The_Wizard_of_Oz_(1939_film).

102 Garland, Judy; Bolger, Ray; Haley, Jack; Lahr, Bert, "We're Off to See the Wizard" (lyrics by E. Y. Harburg, music by Harold Arlen), Alfred Publishing Co. Inc., © 1938 (Renewed), Metro-Goldwyn-Mayer Inc., © 1939 (Renewed), Emi Feist Catalog Inc.

103 "The Journey Through Life," https:/livingweldyingwell/resources/the-journry-through-lifr/, ©Living Well Dying Well NSW, 2022.

104 Sandford, Kathryn, https;//www.kathrynsandford.com, ©2022.

105 Sandford, Kathryn, "How to Persevere (and Get Ahead) When the Going Gets Tough," https://lifehack.org/817679/how-to-persevere, ©2022, (Auckland, New Zealand).

106 Zschech, Darlene, "Shout to the Lord," *Shout to the Lord (Hillsong Album)*, lyrics by Darlene Zschech, Hillsong Music Australia, 1993.

107 Courtney, Camerin, "The Power of Praising God," *Today's Christian Woman*, (Darlene Zschech Interview), March 2001.

108 "Shout to the Lord." Lyricsmode© 2018, https://www.lyricsmode.com/lyrics/d/darlene/zschech/shout-to-the-lord.html#35362.

109 Thorn, Jen, "God Keeps His Promises," (Love God Greatly, "Walking in Victory" July 14, 2019), https://lovegodgreatly.com/god-keeps-his-promises.

Chapter 9: The Most Precious Gift of All

110 Paulsen, Michael Stokes, "The Radical Wrongness of Roe," *First Things*, October, 2021: 21–23.

111 Mother Teresa, *Wall Street Journal* ("Notable and Quotable" column), February 25, 1994, P. A14.

112 Kanaat, Robert (R. L. Adams, pen name), "8 Reasons Why Life Is So Precious," https://wanderlustworker.com/8-reasons-why-llife-is-so-precious, 2018.

113 Ibid. "Number 2—There Is a Reason for Every Failure We Experience in Life."

[114] Ibid. "Number 3—Pain Makes Us Stronger and More Aware."

[115] Ibid. "Number 5—Gratitude Is the Pathway to Hope."

[116] Ibid. "Number 7—All of Us Are on Unique Journeys in Life and We Shouldn't Compare Ourselves to Others."

[117] Kanaat, Robert (R. L. Adams), "About This Blog," https://wanderlustworker,com/about-this-blog/, 2014.

[118] Vocabulary.com, definition of "happiness," https;//www.vocabulary.com/dictionary/happiness, 2008.

[119] Wiley, Pete, "The Foundation of Happiness: Bringing to Others by Making Yourself Happy First" https://blocksoflife/foundation, December 7, 2019

About the Author

B art Mercurio's most recent book, *The Light Always Shines in the Dark*, is an inspiring and eye-opening follow-up to his first book, *At Last I Open My Heart*, in which he shared the true story of his forty-year struggle with addiction. With no plan to retire soon, Bart continues to pursue his lifelong passion to write and has now begun work on his third book, *The Bits of a Broken Heart*.

Presently making his home in Elyria, Ohio, Bart remains very active. Since 1993, he has successfully managed his own business as a tax specialist and a certified trainer in tax education. Gifted with an exceptional memory, he is a connoisseur of crosswords, a fanatical trivia enthusiast, and a relentless reader with a never-ending thirst to seek more and more knowledge and learn new skills. He rarely slows down and is currently teaching himself to play the musical keyboard.

For the past twenty years, Bart has shared his powerful testimony with small and large groups alike. In his straightforward and down-to-earth style, he genuinely presents a positive message of inspiration and hope to his audiences and readers. A native of Cleveland, Ohio, he is the proud, loving father of two adult children, a daughter and a son, and the grandfather of five. To learn more about Bart's availability to share his testimony, you may contact him at mercuriob@ymail.com.

www.ingramcontent.com/pod-product-compliance
Lightning Source LLC
Chambersburg PA
CBHW022011150726
47990CB00002B/600